Animal
Anatomy and Physiology

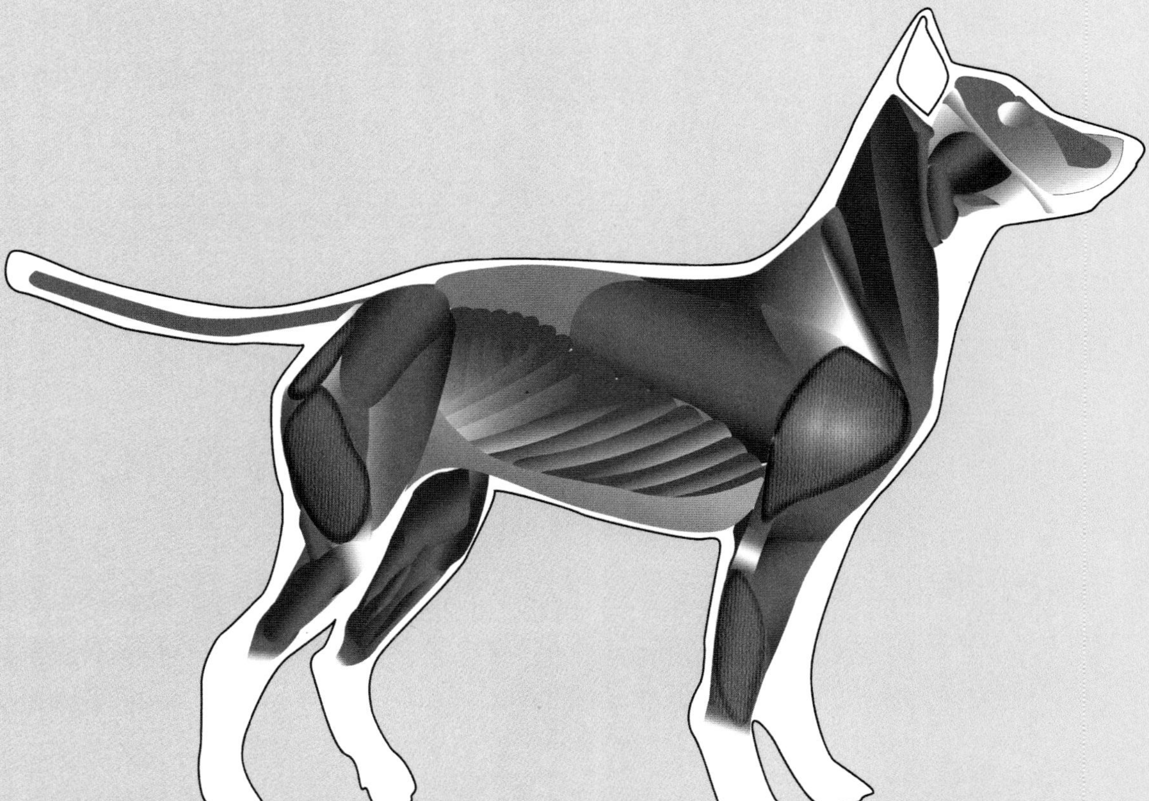

WILLIAM JOHNSTON, DVM

DARNLEY PUBLISHING GROUP

Legal deposit – Bibliothèque et Archives nationales du Québec, 2010
Legal deposit – Library and Archives Canada, 2010

ISBN 978-2-923623-31-3

Printed in Canada

Catalog Number: TCEC2

Author: William Johnston, D.V.M.

Instructional Designer and Reviewer: Claude P. Major, Ph.D.

Technical Writers: Alison Piper, M.A. (Ed. Tech.)
Krista E. Garver

Copy Editor: Krista E. Garver

Project Manager: Francine Hébert, M.Ed.

Design and Layout: Rasha Razzak
Jason Carrière

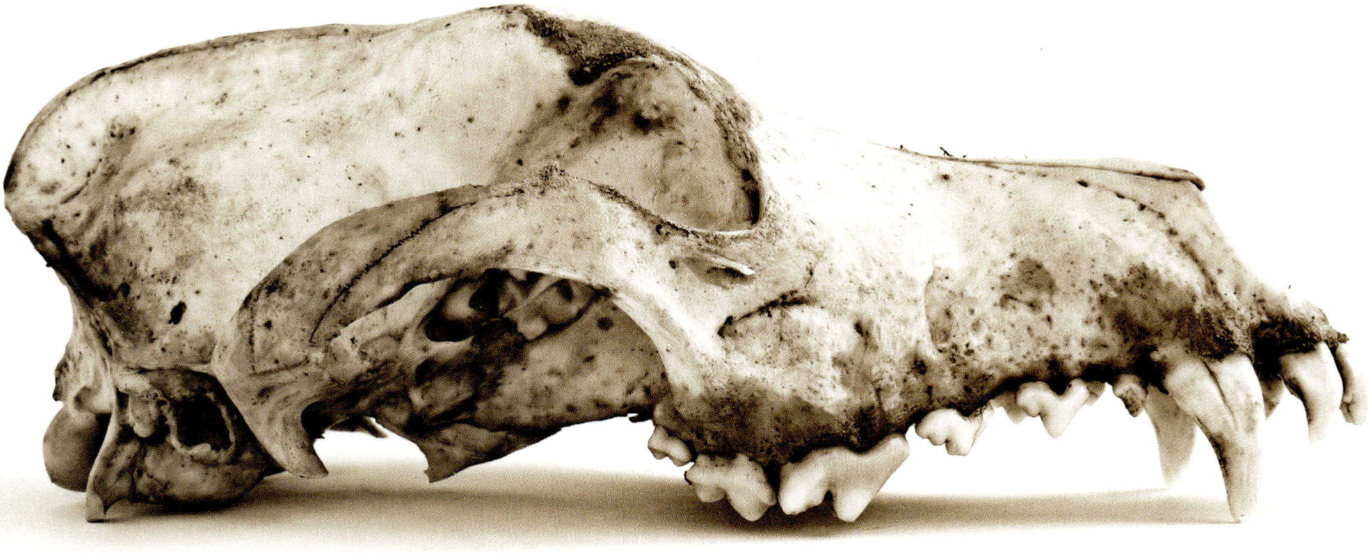

Dog Skull

Table of Contents

Table of Contents

Table of Contents

Chapter 4

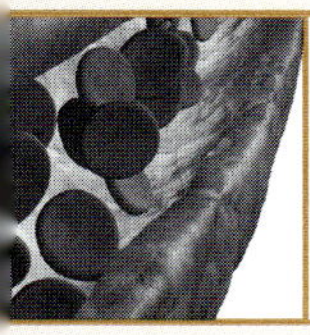

Chapter 5

Table of Contents

Chapter 6

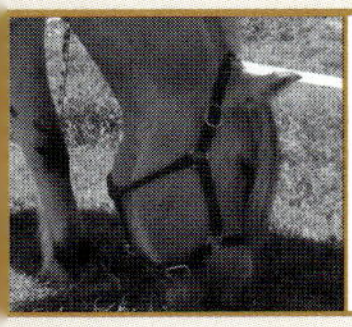

Chapter 7

Table of Contents

Chapter 8

Chapter 9

Table of Contents

Chapter 10 The Nervous and Sensory Systems 157

Table of Contents

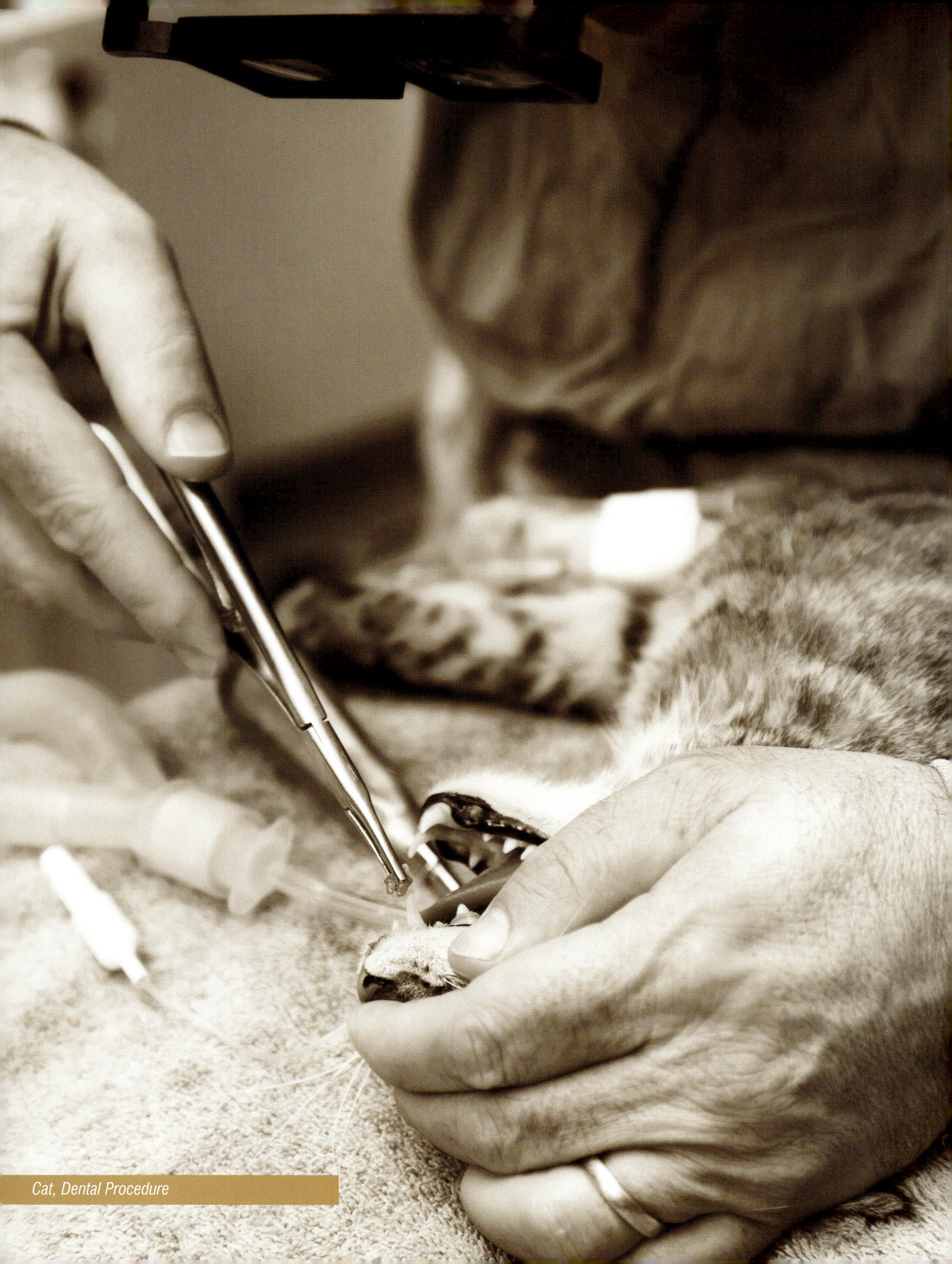

Cat, Dental Procedure

Introduction

As you are about to discover by reading this book, an animal's body is an amazing machine. The various parts of the body must work together to maintain the animal's health and well-being. For example, the cardiovascular, blood, and respiratory systems team up to ensure that body tissues have a constant supply of oxygenated blood. The skeleton and skeletal muscles collaborate to provide structure and support and allow movement. Together, the digestive and urinary systems are responsible for eliminating solid and liquid body wastes.

This book will build upon the knowledge you gained from reading *The Veterinary Assistant Career and Medical Terminology*. Much of the information from the previous book will be useful here, and you will be referred back to that text frequently to review that information. This book deals specifically with the anatomy and physiology of domestic animals: dogs, cats, horses, cattle, swine, sheep, and goats. Anatomy deals with the form and structure of the body and its parts. Physiology deals with the functions of the body and its parts.

Since the body's parts and their functions are interrelated, this book looks at anatomy and physiology together. The combination of these two subjects will give you a complete picture of what the different parts of the body look like, where they are located, how they work, and what they do.

As a veterinary care professional, you will need to develop an understanding of how animals' bodies are put together and how they work. You will see that while normal anatomy and physiology are critical to an animal's health and survival, abnormalities in body structure and functioning often result in disease. These abnormalities will eventually manifest themselves in symptoms of illness, making veterinary care necessary. Having a basic knowledge of normal anatomy and physiology will help you to detect possible problems and monitor an animal's health and recovery during veterinary treatment.

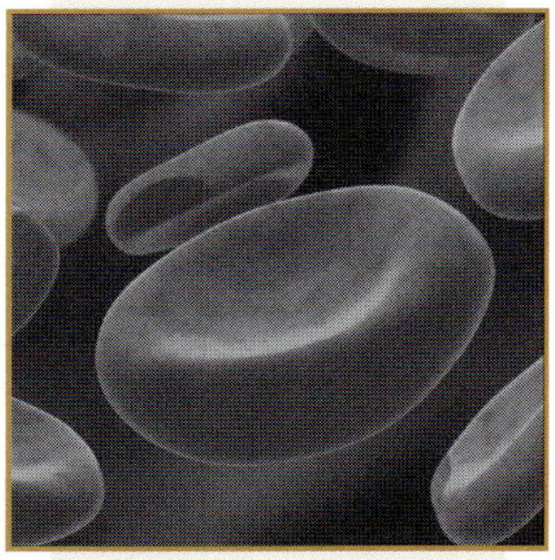

Chapter Breakdown

Chapter 1, "Introduction to Animal Anatomy and Physiology," will introduce you to anatomy and physiology basics. These include the cell, the body's smallest building block, the various types of tissues found within body organs and structures, and the body's major organs and organ systems. Within an animal's body, organs are arranged into systems linked by a common function, such as the digestive, cardiovascular, and respiratory systems. These systems are described in detail in chapters 2 through 11.

Chapter 2, "The Skin," explains the structure and function of the skin layers and accessory skin structures, which include hair, claws, horns, and hooves.

Chapter 3, "The Musculoskeletal System," covers the locations and functions of the major bones, joints, and muscle groups found throughout the body. It also explains how bones and muscles work together with tendons and muscles to allow movement.

In chapter 4, "The Cardiovascular System and the Blood," you will read about the structure and function of the heart, blood vessels, and blood.

Chapter 5, "The Lymphatic System," explains the important role this system plays in the body's immune system response to foreign invaders by mobilizing various types of white blood cells to attack them.

The respiratory system provides oxygen to an animal's bloodstream so that oxygenated blood can always reach its tissues and cells. It also transports carbon dioxide away from an animal's cells as a waste product, which is expelled from the body when an animal exhales. Chapter 6, "The Respiratory System," explains how these processes occur.

Digestion is a complex process in which food is digested and broken down chemically into the basic nutrients needed to fuel body processes and provide energy. Chapter 7, "The Digestive System," explains this process and describes how diet affects the structure and function of domestic animals' digestive systems.

Chapter 8, "The Urinary System," describes how urine is formed, stored, and eliminated from the body. It also explains the kidneys' important role in removing waste products from the blood.

Chapter 9, "The Reproductive System," covers the anatomical parts and processes related to domestic animals' reproductive systems. It also provides key information on the breeding cycles of animals.

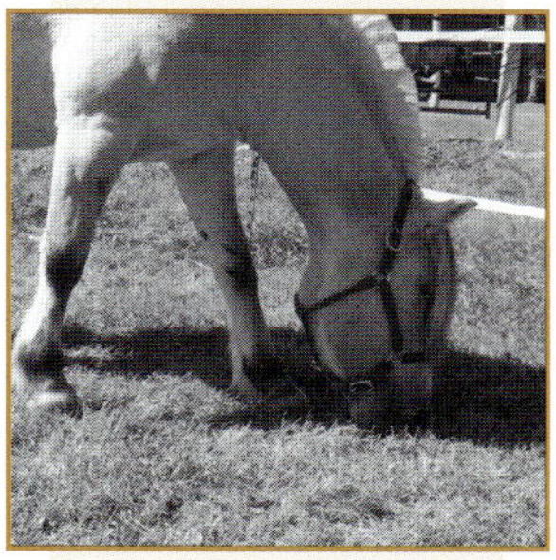

An animal's sensory organs and nerves allow it to perceive and communicate with its environment through its senses. Chapter 10, "The Nervous and Sensory Systems," explains how this occurs. It also covers the various parts of the nervous system and their function, including the brain, spinal column, and peripheral nerves found throughout the body.

The endocrine system shares responsibility for coordination and control of the body with the nervous system. It regulates metabolism, growth, development, maturation, and tissue function, and helps determine mood. You will read about the endocrine system's important role in regulating body functions in chapter 11.

Special Features

This book includes the following features to help you to understand and remember the material:

Highlights of the Chapter. This section is included at the beginning of each chapter to introduce the topics to be covered.

Diagrams and Illustrations. Labeled illustrations and diagrams of body systems and parts are included in each chapter to help you visualize animal anatomy.

Tables. Key information on animal anatomy and physiology is provided in table format, making it quick and easy to read.

Summary. All chapters end with a short summary to reinforce and help you remember key points and concepts.

Key Terms. Key terms introduced in the text are briefly defined at the end of each chapter. If you forget what a term means, you can look it up in this section.

What Do You Remember? Review questions at the end of each chapter test your knowledge and understanding of the content. An answer key is provided at the end of the book.

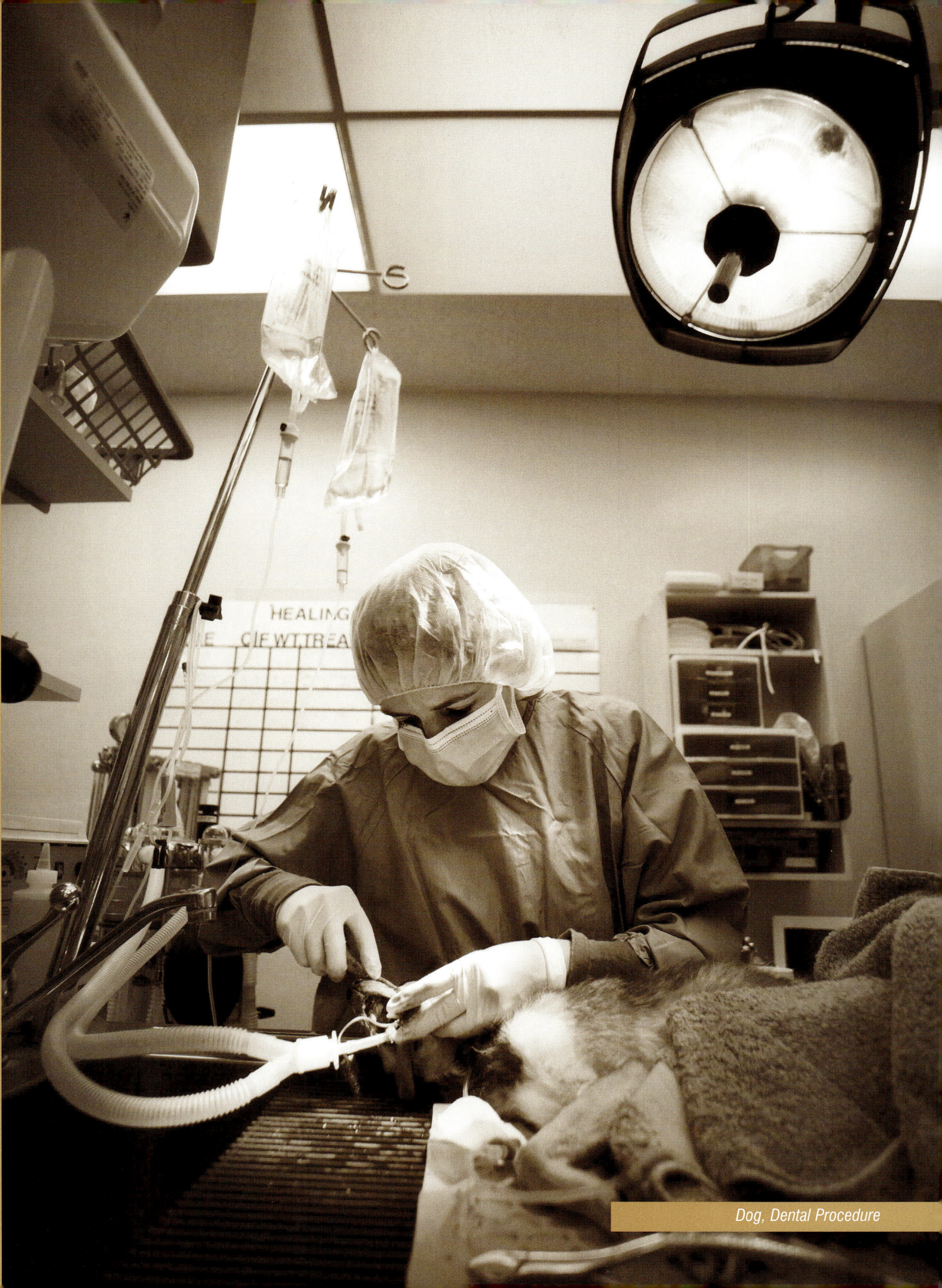

Dog, Dental Procedure

Red Blood Cells

Chapter 1

Introduction to Animal Anatomy and Physiology

Highlights of the Chapter

- The functions of cells
- The four types of living tissue found in domestic animals
- The major organ systems of domestic animals
- The body cavities that contain domestic animals' organs
- Homeostasis—the process by which an animal maintains its body systems in a state of equilibrium

Introduction

Anatomy is the study of body structure, while physiology is the study of body function. The structure of a body part is always related to its function, which is why anatomy and physiology must be studied together.

There are four main levels on which a domestic animal's anatomy and physiology may be examined:

Cells

Tissues

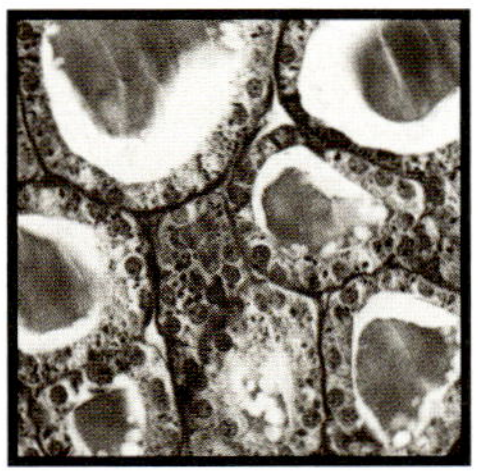

Organs

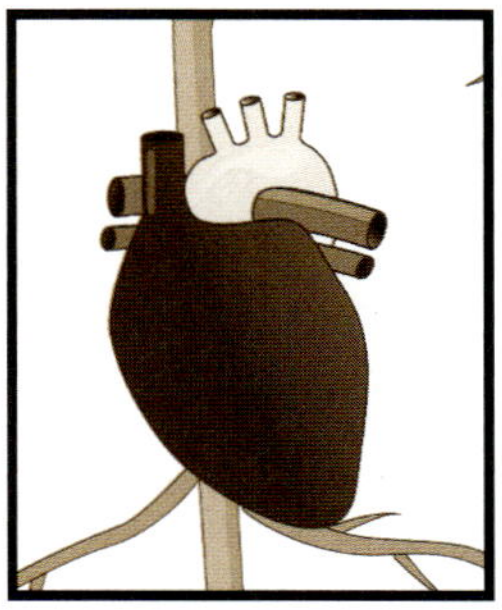

Body Systems

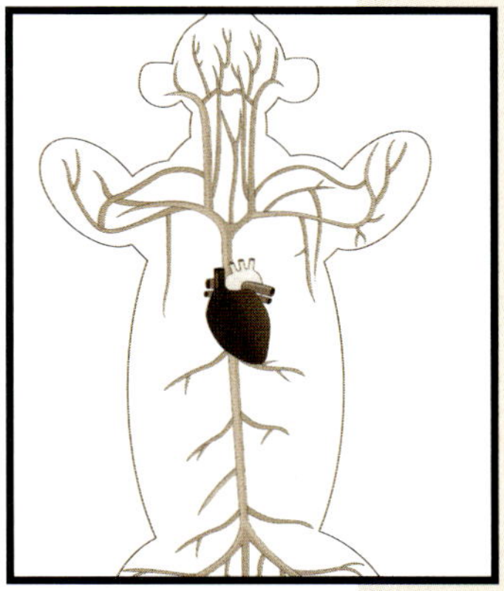

This chapter will briefly review each of these levels as they relate to the basic structure and organization of an animal's body. For a more detailed presentation of the information, see *The Veterinary Assistant Career and Medical Terminology* (chapter 6, "Body Structure and Organization").

Cells

Figure 1.1 Parts of a Cell

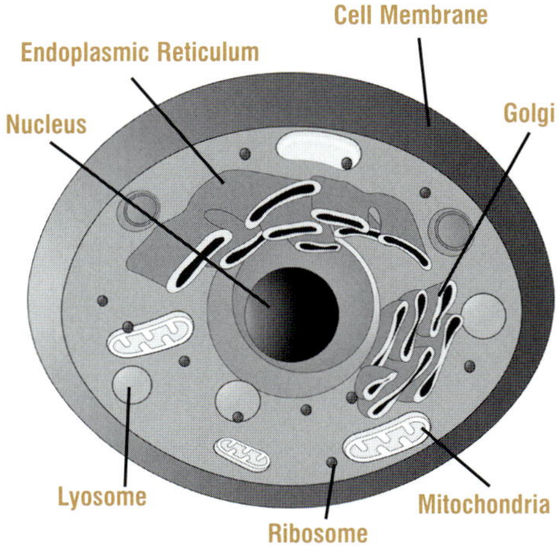

The cell is the basic building block of all living organisms. Cells contain "machinery" that carries out many of the functions necessary for survival. Cells have many parts, which are responsible for all of these functions. Figure 1.1 shows the major components that make up cells.

The heart of the cell is the nucleus, which contains genetic information in the form of DNA, as well as all of the information needed to make proteins. This information is contained in strands of RNA.

The other parts of the cell are smaller structures that are responsible for its regular operations, including respiration, nutrition, excretion of waste, and reproduction. These other parts, called organelles, include the mitochondria (the "power plant" of the cell), ribosomes (involved in making proteins), and the endoplasmic reticulum (involved in making and transporting substances inside the cell).

Finally, all cells have a semi-permeable membrane that regulates what moves in and out of the cell walls.

The Types of Tissue

There are four major tissue types found in domestic animals:

- Epithelial tissue
- Connective tissue
- Muscle tissue
- Neural tissue

Epithelial Tissue

Epithelial tissue covers all body surfaces. It includes the skin as well as the lining of many organs. There are several different types of epithelial tissue, each of which plays a particular role depending on the organ it is covering. For example, the stomach is lined with simple columnar epithelial tissue.

Figure 1.2 Epithelial Tissue

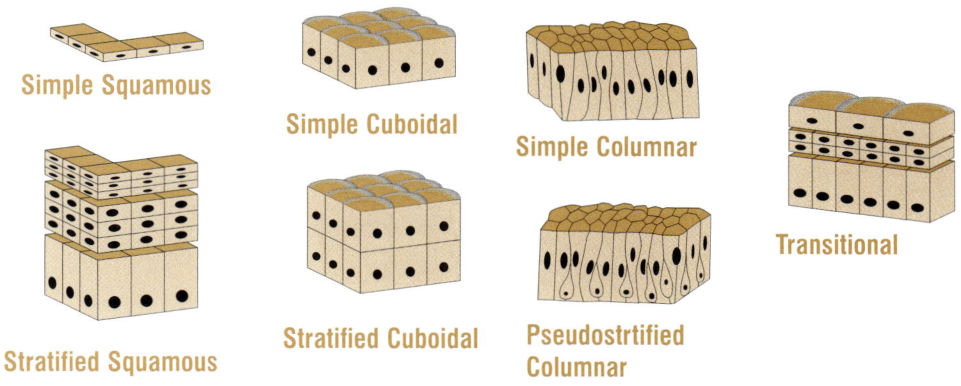

Connective Tissue

Connective tissue is responsible for connecting structures together as well as providing support and protection.

There are five main types of connective tissue:

- Fibrous connective tissue, such as tendons and ligaments
- Elastic connective tissue, for example, the tissue that lines the walls of blood vessels
- Loose connective tissue, which includes adipose, or fatty, tissue
- Cartilage, which is found in joints
- Bone

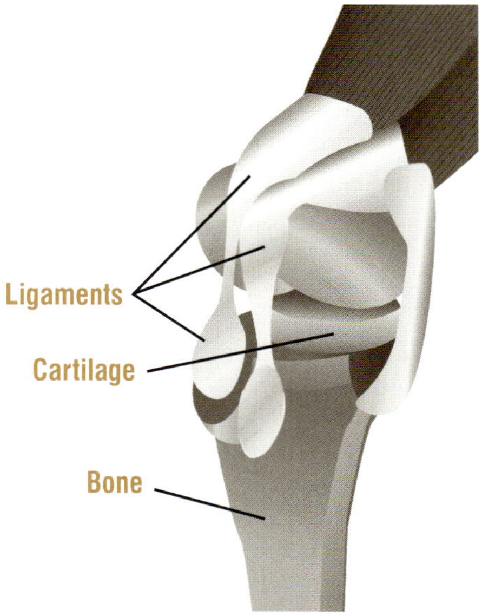

Figure 1.3 Connective Tissue

Muscle Tissue

Figure 1.4 Muscle Tissue

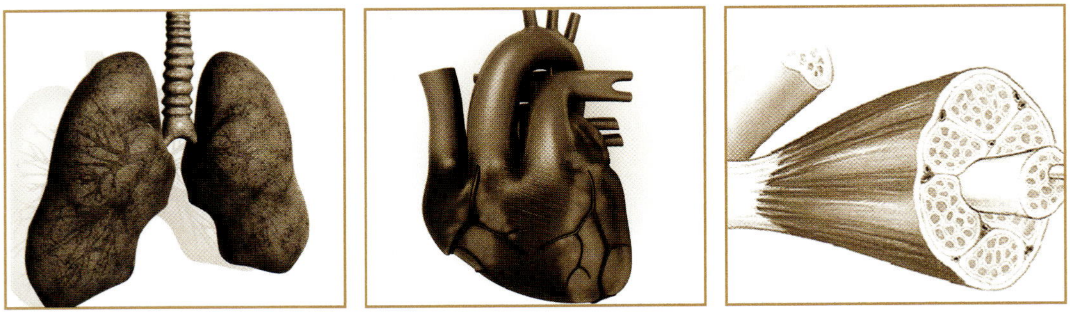

Muscles are necessary for animals to move as well as for many of their body systems to work properly.

There are three types of muscle tissue:

- Smooth muscle is responsible for muscular activity that is unconscious and involuntary, such as breathing.
- Cardiac muscle is found only the heart and is responsible for keeping the heart beating.
- Skeletal muscle constitutes an animal's leg muscles, abdominal muscles, and so on. It contributes to voluntary movement. The musculoskeletal system will be covered in more detail in chapter 3.

Neural Tissue

Finally, neural tissue is found in the brain, spinal cord, and peripheral nerves. It is composed of neurons, which are responsible for communication between different parts of the body, and

Figure 1.5 Neural Tissue

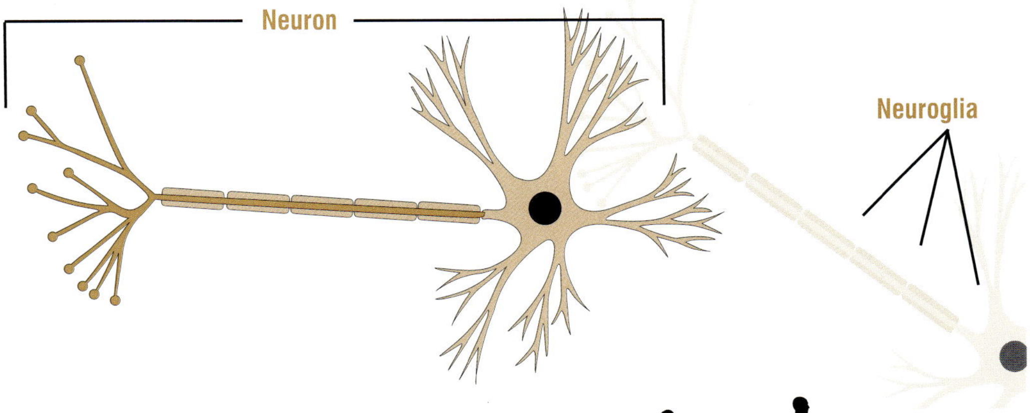

neuroglia, which provide support and protection. See chapter 10 for more information about the nervous system.

Body Cavities

Domestic animals have two main body cavities, which contain and protect their internal organs.

Each of the main body cavities is divided into smaller cavities:

- The dorsal cavity includes the cranial cavity and the spinal cavity.
- The ventral cavity is divided into the thoracic (chest) cavity, the abdominal cavity, and the pelvic cavity.

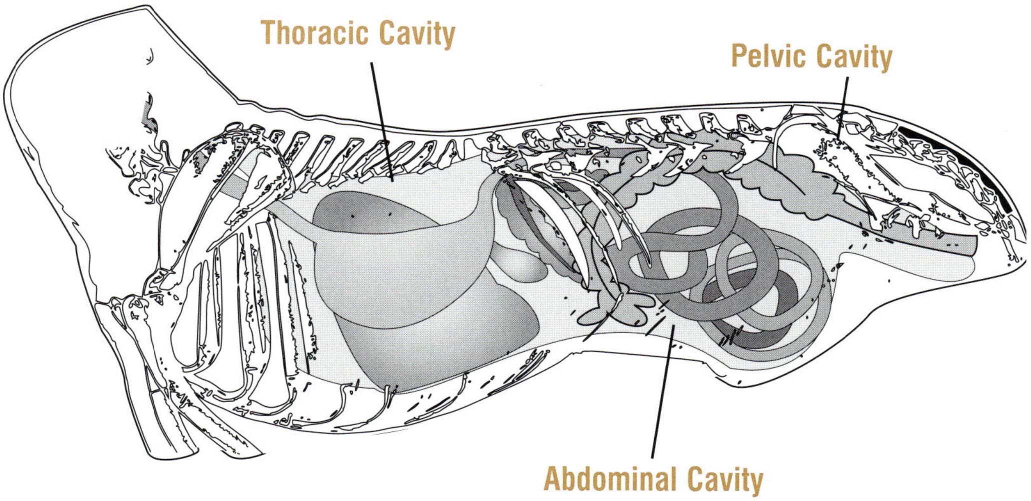

Figure 1.6 The Ventral Cavity of a Domestic Dog

Body Systems of Domestic Animals

Finally, all of an animal's organs are arranged into body systems, which are linked by a common function. Table 1.1 lists the major body systems and describes their organs, functions, and locations. The rest of this book will focus on explaining these body systems in greater detail.

Table 1.1 Body Systems of Domestic Animals

Body System	Includes	Major Function	Location
Blood or hematopoietic	Blood and blood-forming organs	Provides the body's cells with oxygen, nutrients, and essential chemicals	All tissues throughout the body
Cardiovascular	Heart and blood vessels	Provides continual circulation of the blood Transports nutrients, wastes, and gases	Thoracic cavity
Digestive	Mouth, tongue, pharynx, esophagus, stomach, intestines, gall bladder, liver, and pancreas	Processes food and allows the body to absorb nutrients, minerals, vitamins, and water	Abdominal and pelvic cavities
Endocrine	Pituitary gland, pineal gland, parathyroid glands, thyroid gland, thymus, pancreas, adrenal glands, ovaries, and testes	Provides chemical control over body functions through hormones. The endocrine system controls the following: ■ Water metabolism ■ Growth and development ■ Metabolism ■ Composition of bones and blood ■ Sexual maturity	Cranial, thoracic, abdominal, and pelvic cavities, and scrotum (in males)

Table 1.1 Body Systems of Domestic Animals (continued)

Body System	Includes	Major Function	Location
Integumentary (skin)	Skin and associated structures, such as hair, claws, and paw pads	Protects the body from environmental hazards and helps control body temperature	Surface of the body and inner skin layers
Lymphatic	Vessels and glands responsible for immunity	Defends against infection and disease	Lymph glands and nodes throughout the body
Musculoskeletal	Bones, muscles, and connective tissues	Provides for the structure, support, and movement of the body	Bones and skeletal muscles throughout the body
Nervous	Brain, spinal cord, peripheral nerves, and sense organs	Directs immediate responses to stimuli by coordinating the activities of other organ systems	Cranial and spinal cavities Peripheral nerves throughout the body
Reproductive	Reproductive organs, including the ovaries and uterus in the female and the testicles, penis, and prostate gland in the male	Produces sex cells (eggs in female, sperm in males) and sex hormones	Pelvic cavity (female reproductive organs and prostate gland in the male) Outside of the body in the pelvic region (male reproductive organs)
Respiratory	Airway running from the nose to the lungs	Takes in oxygen and expels carbon dioxide	Nasal passages, neck, and thoracic cavity
Urinary	Kidneys and urinary bladder	Filters blood to remove waste products and eliminates liquid waste from the body	Pelvic cavity

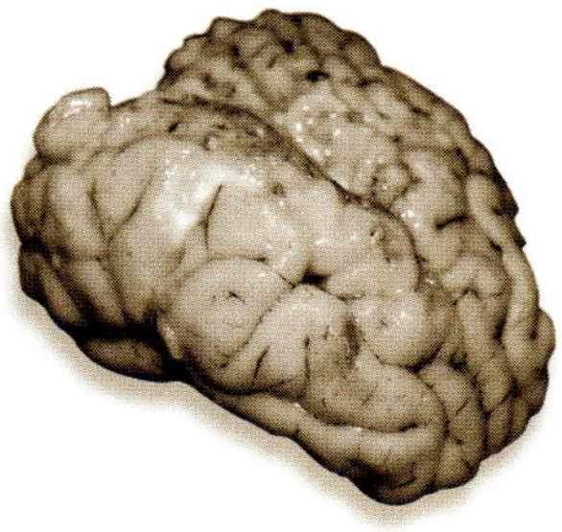

Homeostasis

The process by which an animal maintains its internal equilibrium by adjusting its physiological processes is called homeostasis. This requires the coordination of many physiological processes that involve various body systems. These are called homeostatic mechanisms. Examples of homeostatic mechanisms include the regulation of body temperature, respiratory rate, blood pH and pressure, heart rate, levels of blood glucose and body water, and electrolyte concentrations.

How does homeostasis work? When something goes wrong in the body, receptors in the body, such as nerves, send a message to the brain. The brain determines the appropriate response to the stimulus, sending a signal to muscles or organ systems to effect change in the opposite direction to the output. Equilibrium is maintained because the initial problem is corrected through internal controls.

Let's look at an example involving a dog with acute diarrhea. The dog's body is losing fluid and becoming dehydrated. To compensate, the brain triggers the pituitary gland to release an antidiuretic hormone into the bloodstream, stimulating the kidneys to secrete less water in urine. The concentration of urine increases as water is retained in the body. Eventually, thirst centers within the brain are activated, which stimulates the dog to drink water. This will allow body systems to return to normal.

Homeostatic imbalance is a disturbance of the body's natural equilibrium, and it can lead to a variety of diseases and conditions. Diabetes, dehydration, hypoglycemia, and hyperglycemia all result from a homeostatic imbalance: they are caused by the presence of too much or too little of a particular substance in the body. For example, dehydration results from having too little water in the system, and hyperglycemia results from too much sugar.

As the body ages, it becomes less efficient at controlling homeostatic processes, which can lead to an increased risk of illness. For example, older animals are not as effecient as younger animals in regulating their energy and water metablism.

Summary

Cells are the structural and functional units of all living things. A tissue is made up of many cells of a particular type.

Domestic animals' bodies contain four main types of tissue: epithelial, connective, muscle, and neural. Epithelial tissue is found in the outer layers of skin as well as in the lining of many organs. Connective tissue is found in bones, cartilage, tendons, and ligaments. Neural tissue is found in the brain, spinal cord, and peripheral nerves. There are three types of muscle tissue: smooth muscle, cardiac muscle, and skeletal muscle.

An organ is a collection of different tissues that work together to perform a particular function. Organs include the stomach, liver, kidneys, and brain. A body system is a collection of parts, structures, organs, and tissues that all contribute to a common function. The body systems of domestic animals are the following: blood (hematopoietic), cardiovascular, digestive, endocrine, integumentary, lymphatic, musculoskeletal, nervous, reproductive, respiratory, and urinary.

Domestic animals' organs and body systems are contained in two main body cavities: the dorsal cavity, which is divided into the cranial and spinal cavities, and the ventral cavity, which comprises the thoracic, abdominal, and pelvic cavities.

Homeostasis is the process by which an animal maintains its internal equilibrium by adjusting its physiological processes. Homeostatic mechanisms include the regulation of body temperature, respiratory rate, heart rate, and blood glucose. Much disease results from a disturbance of homeostasis. For example, diabetes, dehydration, hypoglycemia, and gout all result from the presence of an increased amount of a particular substance.

Key Terms

Term	Definition
Abdominal cavity	The body cavity containing the liver, stomach, small intestines, part of the large intestine, the kidneys, and the pancreas.
Anatomy	The study of internal and external body structures. An animal's anatomy includes its skeleton, muscles, skin, and internal organs.
Body system	A collection of structures, organs, and tissues that are linked by their contribution to a common function, such as the respiratory and digestive systems.
Bone	A dense, rigid type of connective tissue that provides support for muscles and protects body tissues and organs.
Cartilage	A more rigid form of connective tissue found in joints between bones and in the ribs, nose, and sternum. Cartilage protects bone and helps joints to move while absorbing some of the forces within them.
Cells	The basic units of all living things which form the complex tissue and organs that make up an animal's body.
Connective tissue	The tissue that connects structures together, providing support and protection. Connective tissue includes bone, cartilage, tendons, and ligaments.
Cranial cavity	The body cavity that contains the brain.
Diabetes	A disease characterized by an inability to process sugars in the diet due to a decrease in, or total absence of, insulin production.
DNA	The hereditary material of genes, contained in cells.

Key Terms

Term	Definition
Dorsal cavity	The body cavity subdivided into the cranial and spinal cavities.
Epithelial tissue	The tissue covering all body surfaces, inside and out, including the outer layers of skin.
Gout	An acute form of arthritis that causes severe pain and swelling in the joints.
Homeostasis	The process by which an animal maintains its internal equilibrium by adjusting its physiological processes. Various sensing, feedback, and control mechanisms function to effect this steady state.
Hyperglycemia	A condition in which blood glucose levels reach abnormally high levels, which is often a clinical sign of diabetes.
Hypoglycemia	A condition in which blood glucose concentrations fall below a level necessary to properly support the body's need for energy and stability. Commonly called low blood sugar.
Muscle tissue	Elastic tissue that can contract and relax to change its length. Muscles allow animals to move, cause their hearts to beat, allow their lungs to expand and relax, and move food through their digestive systems.
Neural tissue	Tissue composed of neurons and found in the brain, spinal cord, and peripheral nerves.
Neuroglia	Cells that provide support, protection, oxygen, and nutrients for neurons.
Neurons	Highly specialized nerve cells that transmit electrical impulses to all areas of the body.

Key Terms

Term	Definition
Organ	A collection of different tissues that work together to perform a particular function.
Pelvic cavity	The body cavity containing the bladder, the final section of the large intestine, and the reproductive organs of the female or the prostate gland of the male.
Peripheral nerves	Nerves outside of the brain and spinal cord.
Physiology	The study of how animals perform their vital functions.
RNA	A molecule that serves as a template for protein synthesis in the body.
Spinal cavity	The body cavity that contains the spinal cord.
Thoracic cavity	The body cavity containing the heart and lungs.
Tissue	A collection of cells in which one type of cell predominates.
Ventral cavity	The ventral cavity is subdivided into the thoracic, abdominal, and pelvic cavities.

What Do You Remember?

Answer key on page 199

Exercise 1–1

1. __________ are the basic building blocks of all living things.

a. Cells
b. Tissues
c. Organs
d. Systems

2. Which body cavity contains the bladder?

a. dorsal
b. abdominal
c. pelvic
d. thoracic

3. Which of the following body cavities is found in the dorsal cavity?

a. spinal
b. thoracic
c. abdominal
d. pelvic

4. Tendons and ligaments are made of _______________.

a. fibrous connective tissue
b. cartilage
c. skeletal muscle
d. smooth muscle

5. _____________ is found in joints between bones.

a. Fibrous connective tissue
b. Cartilage
c. Skeletal muscle
d. Smooth muscle

Answer key on page 199

What Do You Remember?

6. The outer layers of skin are made of ________________.

a. fibrous connective tissue
b. elastic connective tissue
c. loose connective tissue
d. epithelial tissue

Exercise 1–2

Match each body system with its major function.

1. hematopoietic
2. cardiovascular
3. digestive
4. endocrine
5. integumentary
6. lymphatic
7. musculoskeletal
8. nervous
9. reproductive
10. respiratory
11. urinary

a. provides chemical control over body functions through hormones
b. defends against infection and disease
c. takes in oxygen and expels carbon dioxide
d. processes food and allows the body to absorb nutrients, minerals, vitamins, and water
e. provides the body's cells with oxygen, nutrients, and essential chemicals
f. directs immediate responses to stimuli by coordinating the activities of other systems
g. provides for the structure, support, and movement of the body
h. transports nutrients, wastes, and gases
i. filters blood to remove waste products and eliminates liquid waste from the body
j. produces sex cells
k. protects the body from environmental hazards and helps control body temperature

Goat

Constantine, Norwegian Fjord

CHAPTER 2

The Skin and Accessory Structures

Highlights of the Chapter

- The two layers of skin
- Accessory structures—hair, claws, hooves, and horns
- The function of skin glands
- The role of skin and hair in regulating an animal's body temperature
- How skin heals and repairs itself

Introduction

The skin has many functions and is a very complex organ. It can be described as the body's largest sensory organ. It contains specialized nerve cells that can detect touch, pain, and pressure, helping to protect the animal from injury and harm.

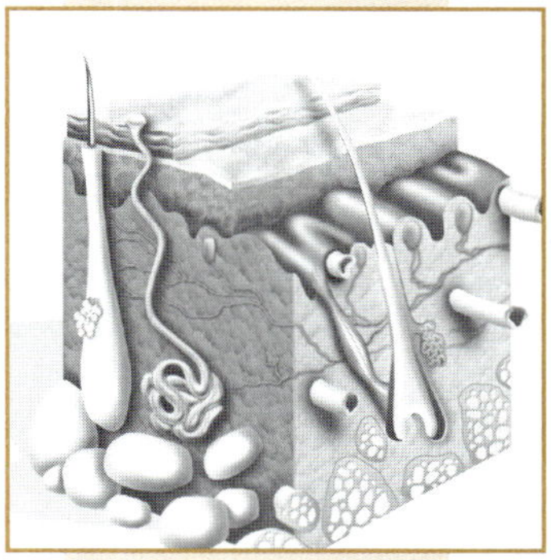

The skin provides a physical barrier that prevents many organisms that cause disease from entering the body. These include bacteria, viruses, fungi, and environmental toxins. The skin also provides an impermeable layer that protects against water loss and the absorption of water.

The skin, together with accessory structures (hair and claws or hooves) and skin glands is called the "integumentary system."

The Two Layers of Skin

An animal's skin has two layers: the epidermis and the dermis. Following is a description of the structure (anatomy) and function (physiology) of these layers and their tissues.

The Epidermis

The outer epidermis is composed of epithelial tissue and is the thinnest of the two skin layers. It has no blood or nerves in it. This layer of skin provides a protective barrier against disease-causing organisms and prevents some chemicals from being absorbed into the body.

The surface of the epidermis is continuously sloughed off during the animal's lifetime. Cells at the base of the epidermis continually divide and push the cells above them upward. As these cells move, they die and become the dry flaky scales that fall off the skin surface.

Figure 2.1 Skin Cell Cycle

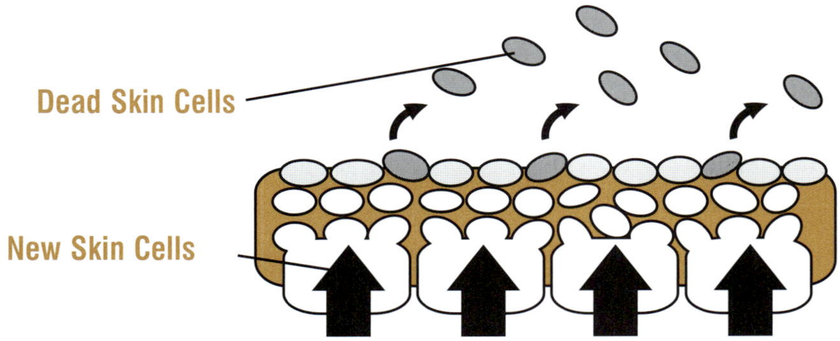

When exposed to ultraviolet light from the sun, the cells of the epidermis produce vitamin D3. This vitamin is essential for the absorption of dietary calcium and phosphorus, which enable bone growth and maintenance. Animals need daily exposure to sunlight to develop and maintain healthy bones. The epidermis also contains melanocytes, or black cells, which absorb light to protect deeper tissues from harmful effects of the sun.

The Dermis

The dermis is the thickest of the two skin layers. It is made of elastic connective tissue and provides most of the skin's structural strength. The dermis contains capillaries, sensory nerves, and skin glands.

Figure 2.2 Layers of the Skin

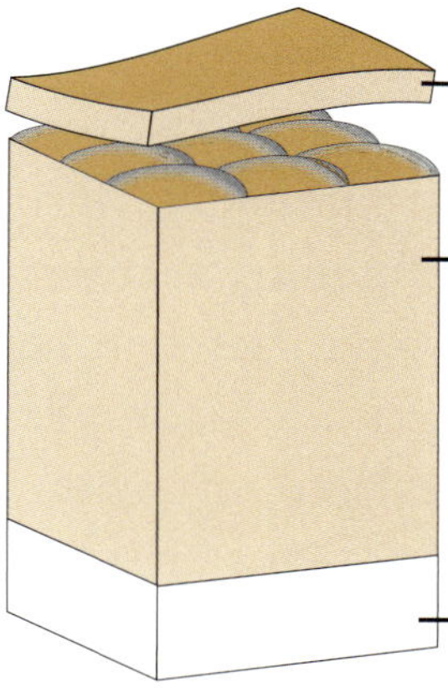

The Subcutaneous Layer

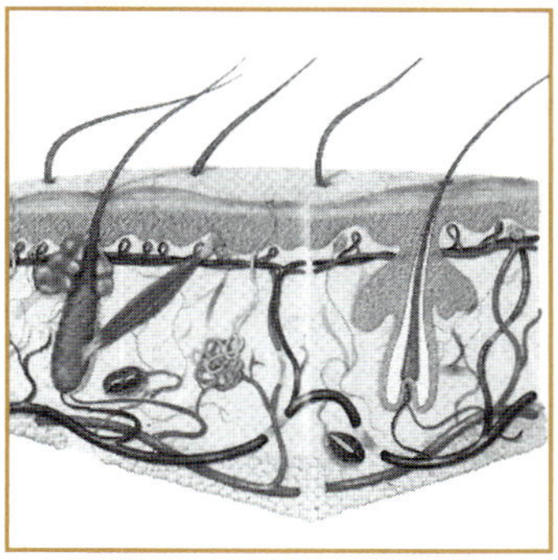

The subcutaneous layer, or hypodermis, lies beneath the dermis. It is not part of the skin, but rather it is composed of adipose tissue and loose connective tissues. The subcutaneous layer is attached to the skin as well as to underlying tissues and organs.

The subcutaneous layer acts as a storage depot for fat and contains large blood vessels that supply the skin. The subcutaneous layer of fat can become excessive in obese animals or depleted in animals that are undernourished.

The Skin Glands

Found in the dermis, the skin glands include sebaceous, sweat, and mammary glands. Sebaceous glands secrete an oily substance called sebum into hair follicles. Sebum keeps the skin and fur soft, pliable, and waterproof. Sebum also has some antibacterial and antifungal properties, which reduce the skin's risk of infection. Some sebaceous glands secrete scent markers called pheromones, which domestic animals use to mark their territories and attract mates.

Most domestic animals, including dogs and cats, have a limited number of sweat glands and cannot use sweating to help control their body temperature. The main exception is horses, which have sweat glands all over their body.

In the female animal during pregnancy, mammary gland tissue develops beneath the dermis in preparation for nursing offspring. The production of milk, or lactation, occurs after the animal gives

birth. Milk is secreted through ducts into external openings called teats. Female dogs usually have five pairs of teats, and female cats have four.

Dogs, cats, and many other mammals also have anal sac glands, which have a powerful, foul-smelling secretion. Anal sacs are located at the 9 o'clock and 3 o'clock positions on both sides of the rectum. They are connected to the anus with a single duct and are normally emptied out during defecation or when the animal becomes frightened. Anal sac secretions transfer the animal's unique smell or "personal identification odor," to the environment. It is believed that they are used to mark territory and attract mates.

Accessory Skin Structures

Accessory skin structures include hair, claws, hooves, and horns, which are all made of keratin, a tough structural fibrous protein and attached to the dermis. The dermis found under an animal's nail or hoof is commonly referred to as the "quick."

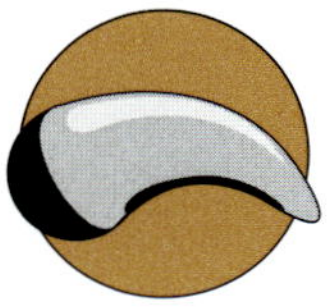

Claws

In dogs and cats, claws protect underlying bones in the foot and provide grip while the animal is walking or running. Claws are also used for grasping, grooming, and digging. In the cat, claws are also weapons of defense.

In many mammals, including cats and dogs, skin structures of the foot also include footpads, which are covered with thick skin and act as protective cushions that protect the weight-bearing surface of the foot. Thick layers of fat and connective tissue form the foundation of footpads.

In dogs and cats, each of the four toes has a digital footpad. There is also a central, heart-shaped pad called the metacarpal pad on each foot and an upper carpal pad on each foreleg. The upper carpal pad provides additional traction when the animal stops or descends a slope. Additional dew claws may also be present on the right side of the foot (see Figure 2.3).

Figure 2.3 Front Paw of a Dog

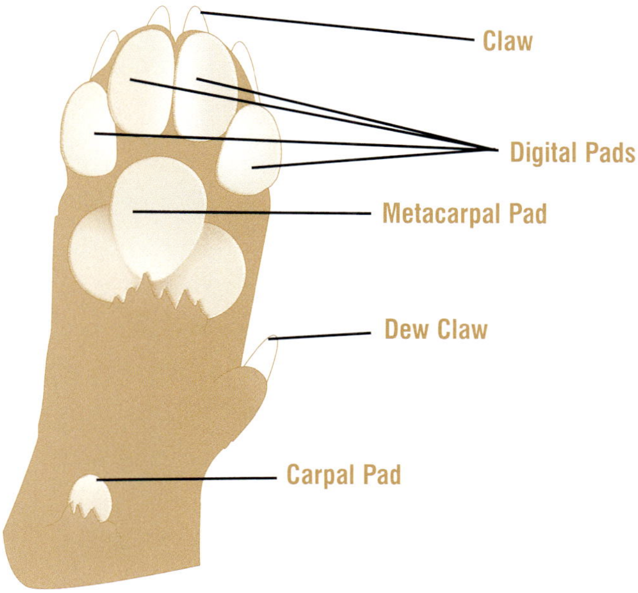

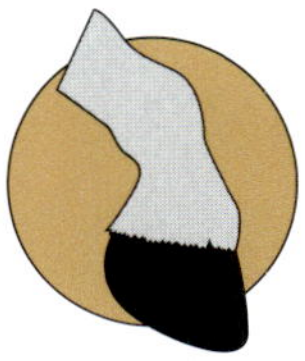

Hooves

In hoofed animals, the hoof consists of a hard or rubbery sole and a hard wall formed by a thick nail rolled around the tip of the toe. The weight of the animal is borne by both the sole and the edge of the hoof wall. Hooves also protect the internal structures of the foot and provide grip on different terrains. They grow continuously and are constantly worn down by use.

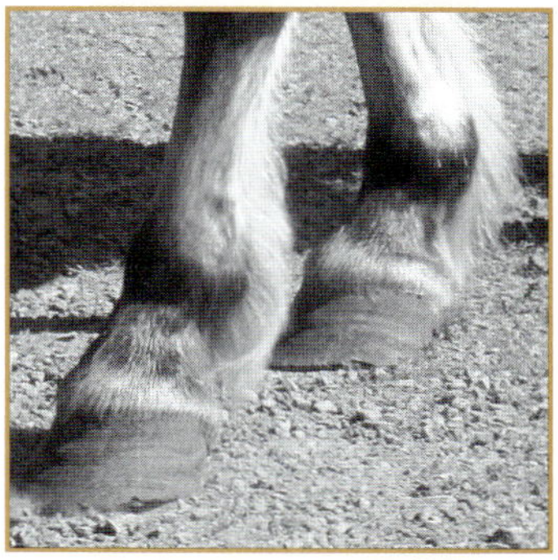

Sheep, goats, cattle, and pigs have a hoof divided into two parts at its distal extremity, called a cloven hoof. They actually have four hooves per foot, each covering a single digit. However, weight is carried only by two digits (the third and fourth). Horses have a single toe covered by a hoof on each foot.

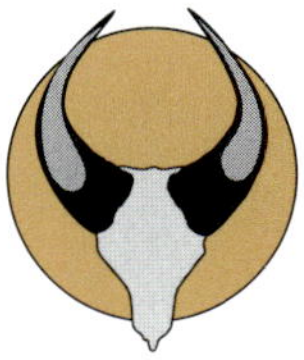

Horns

Consisting of a covering of keratin and other proteins surrounding a core of living bone, horns are found in some ruminant species, including cattle, sheep, and goats. These animals have one or occasionally two pairs of horns, which usually have a curved or spiral shape, often with ridges or fluting. In many species, only the males have horns. Horns start to grow soon after birth and continue to grow throughout the animal's life.

Animals have a variety of uses for horns, including defending themselves from predators and fighting members of their own species for territory, dominance, or mating priority. In addition, horns may be used to root in the soil or strip bark from trees.

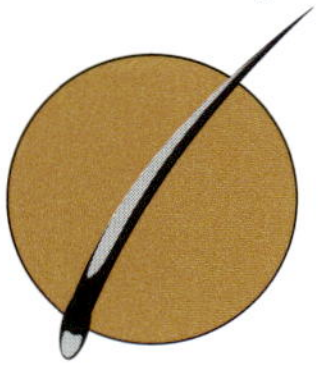

Hair

Hair follicles originate in the dermis and traverse the epidermis to the surface of the skin. Hair begins growing in the hair bulb at the base of the follicle. The hair bulb gives rise to the hair shaft, which is the visible portion of hair. Hair grows up through the surface of the follicle until it penetrates the skin surface. As each hair becomes old and falls out, a replacement hair develops from a new follicle. Sebaceous glands are attached to the hair follicle (see Figure 2.4).

Figure 2.4 Hair Follicle

There are two main types of hairs: guard hairs and undercoat hairs. Guard hairs form the outer layer of the coat. They are thicker, longer, and stiffer than the undercoat hairs. They prevent water from penetrating the undercoat. Undercoat hairs are softer and thinner than the guard hairs. The function of the undercoat is to warm and insulate the body.

Dog breeds such as the Husky have a dense overcoat and undercoat and are able to survive in very cold temperatures. Other breeds, such as the Doberman, have almost no undercoat at all and are less resistant to cold.

In mammals, hair covers most of the skin's surface. The growth of hair, claws, and hooves is continuous. The normal cycle of hair growth and loss occurs on a seasonal basis. Hair growth and loss are strongly affected by the amount of daylight. Most domestic animals begin to shed heavily in the late winter, when the days become longer. They will then start to acquire thicker, more luxurious coats during the fall, when the days become shorter.

The color in hairs is formed from melanin, the same pigment that colors the skin. Coat color may help camouflage animals and sometimes acts to attract the opposite sex.

Special hairs called tactile hairs, which are commonly called whiskers, grow around the nostrils, around the lips, and above the eyes of many mammals, including dogs and cats. Tactile hairs have a sensory function, allowing animals to navigate and find food. They are thicker and stiffer than other types of hair.

Role of Skin and Hair in Regulating Body Temperature

Skin and hair help regulate body temperature within a normal range in a variety of ways. The skin is well supplied with capillaries. In hot temperatures, the capillaries will dilate, or increase in diameter, to conduct heat away from the body's core to the surface, providing a cooling effect. As previously mentioned, sweat glands secrete sweat, which evaporates and cools the skin surface, when an animal is hot or has been exercising strenuously.

Figure 2.5 Capillary Bed

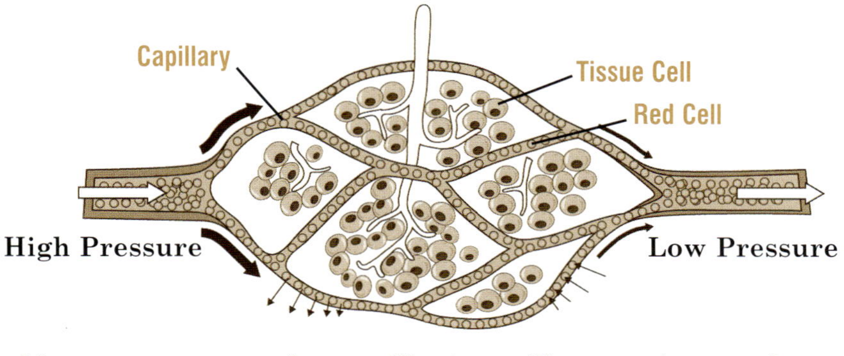

In cold temperatures, the capillaries will constrict, or decrease in diameter, to conserve heat within the body, keeping the animal warm. As a response to cold, an animal's hairs will also become erect, trapping a layer of warm air close to the skin to provide insulation.

The effect is similar to goose bumps in humans, which cause body hairs to stand on end.

Adipose tissue also helps to insulate the body against heat loss.

How Skin Heals and Repairs Itself

Each time a skin wound occurs, the skin at the injured site undergoes a process of tissue healing and repair.

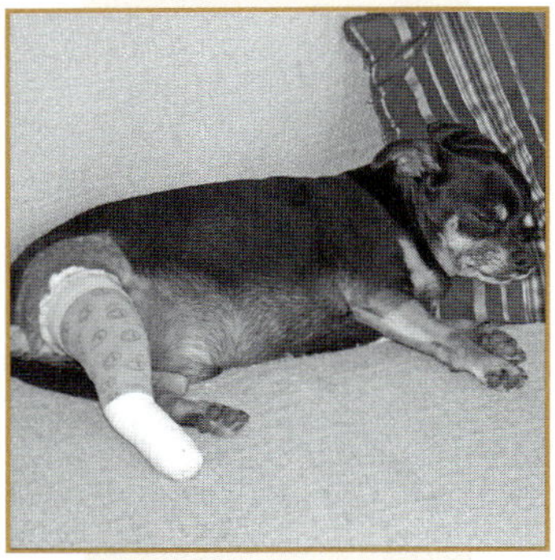

The process has the following four steps:

1. *Injury*. The animal receives a bite, scratch, or cut in the skin.
2. *Inflammation*. Inflammation occurs to quickly limit further damage and help prevent infection. Blood vessels dilate, causing redness in the tissue around the wound. Fluid leaks into the tissue from dilated capillaries, causing swelling and associated pain and tenderness at the injury site. Platelets gather and clump together to slow bleeding and help prevent the invasion of bacteria. A blood clot soon forms at the wound opening, which will later become a scab.
3. *Organization*. Wound repair begins soon after the injury occurs. It continues while dead cells and debris are removed from the wound area. A new, bright pink tissue, called granulation tissue, forms beneath the scab. Granulation tissue is highly resistant to infection.
4. *Regeneration or fibrosis*. Epithelial cells around wound edges proliferate and cover granulation tissue. The scab is pushed off. Slowly, the granulation tissue is completely replaced by fibrous scar tissue, which contracts and helps to pull the wound closed. When regeneration is complete, the underlying scar may or may not be visible, depending on the severity of the injury and the extent of scar formation.

Summary

The skin has many functions and is a complex organ. It is the body's largest sensory organ. It also provides a strong barrier against disease-causing organisms and water loss from the body. The two layers of skin are the outer epidermis and the inner dermis, which contains sensory nerves, skin glands, and hair follicles. Claws, hooves, and horns are also attached to the dermis.

Claws and hooves protect the internal structures of the feet and provide grip to surfaces. Horned animals use their horns to defend themselves against predators and fight members of their own species for territory, dominance, or mating priority. Hair, claws, hooves, and horns are made of keratin and grow continuously throughout an animal's life.

The epidermis of many mammals, such as cats and dogs, includes footpads, which are covered with thick skin. Footpads act as protective cushions that protect the weight-bearing surface of the foot.

Whenever a skin wound occurs, a four-step tissue healing and repair process begins. The first step is the injury itself, followed by inflammation and blood clotting, wound repair with the formation of bright pink granulation tissue, and, finally, regeneration of a permanent layer of new skin.

Key Terms

Term	Definition
Capillary	The smallest of the body's blood vessels, which enables the interchange of water, oxygen, nutrients, and waste materials between blood and surrounding tissues.
Cloven hoof	A hoof split into two parts at its distal extremity. Sheep, goats, cattle, and pigs all have cloven hooves.
Dermis	The inner layer of skin, composed of elastic connective tissue.
Digital pad	The footpad for each of the four toes of a dog or cat.
Epidermis	The outer layer of skin, which is composed of epithelial tissue and has a tightly packed structure that provides a protective barrier.
Fibrous scar tissue	Dense, fibrous connective tissue, which normally forms over a healed cut or wound.
Granulation tissue	The newly formed tissue normally produced in the healing of wounds of soft tissue.
Guard hair	The thicker, longer hair of an animal's outer coat.
Hair bulb	The part of the hair follicle in which hair growth begins.
Hair follicle	The part of the skin that grows hair.
Hair shaft	The visible portion of hair, outside of the body.
Inflammation	The body's response to tissue injury or infection, which typically includes increased blood vessel dilation and permeability, resulting in redness, swelling, heat, and pain.
Integumentary system	The body system comprising skin, hair, skin glands, and claws or hooves.

Key Terms

Term	Definition
Keratin	A tough, insoluble, structural, fibrous protein, which is the building material for hair, claws, hooves, and horns.
Mammary glands	Glands in the dermis that produce and secrete milk in female mammals that are nursing newborns. The mammary glands are part of the female reproductive system.
Melanin	The dark pigment produced by melanocytes that determines skin and hair color.
Melanocytes	Black skin cells found in the epidermis that provide pigmentation to the skin, protecting the deeper tissues from the harmful effects of the sun.
Metacarpal pad	The central, heart-shaped foot pad of a dog or cat.
Pheromones	Scent markers secreted by sebaceous glands, which domestic animals use to mark their territories and attract mates.
Sebaceous gland	Gland found within the dermis that secretes an oily substance called sebum into hair follicles, which helps keep skin and fur soft and waterproof.
Subcutaneous layer	The layer of adipose, or fatty, tissue and loose connective tissues located beneath the dermis.
Sweat gland	Glands found within the dermis that secrete sweat to cool the skin's surface and reduce body temperature.
Undercoat	The thinner, softer hair that warms and insulates an animal's body.
Upper carpal pad	The pad found on the underside of the forelegs of a dog or cat.

Answer key on page 199

What Do You Remember?

1. How many pads does a dog or cat have on each foreleg, assuming that it has dew claws?

a. 4
b. 5
c. 6
d. 7

2. Which of the following is found in the epidermis?

a. melanocyte
b. sebaceous gland
c. sweat gland
d. hair follicle

3. ____________ contains large blood vessels that supply the skin.

a. The dermis
b. The epidermis
c. The subcutaneous layer
d. Adipose tissue

4. Sebum is secreted by the sebaceous glands to _________.

a. lubricate hair
b. stimulate hair growth
c. waterproof hair
d. both a and c

5. The production of which vitamin by the skin is stimulated by ultraviolet light?

a. vitamin A
b. vitamin B12
c. vitamin C
d. vitamin D3

Answer key on page 199

What Do You Remember?

6. **Hair begins growing in the _______________.**

a. hair base
b. hair shaft
c. hair bulb
d. dermis

7. **Which of the following processes related to the integumentary system helps cool the body?**

a. dilation of capillaries
b. constriction of capillaries
c. erection of hairs
d. both a and c

8. **Hair growth and loss are strongly affected by __________.**

a. daylight
b. diet
c. temperature
d. age

Belgian Draught Horse

CHAPTER 3

The Musculoskeletal System

Highlights of the Chapter

- Skeletal and muscle anatomy
- The five categories of bones
- The three main types of joints and their functions
- Fractures and bone healing
- How muscles allow movement

Introduction

The musculoskeletal system is the body's structure and movement system.

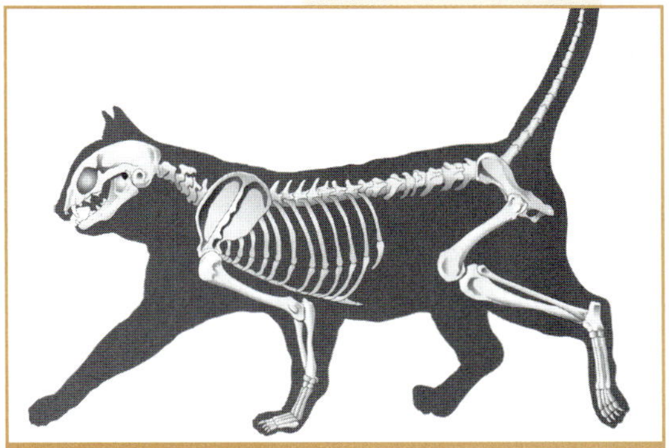
Skeletal System

It is divided into two subsystems:

- The skeletal system
- The muscular system

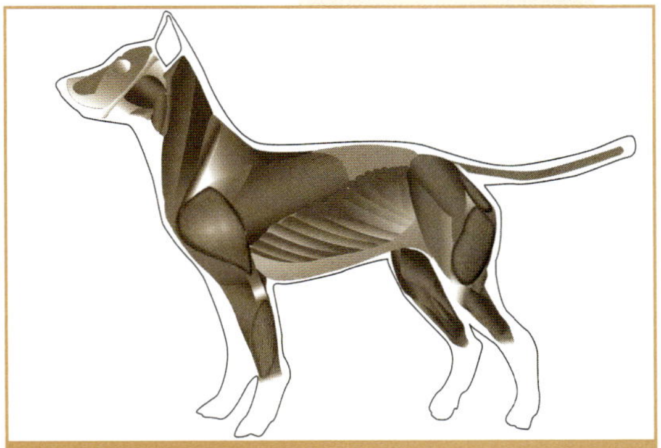
Muscular System

The skeletal system is made up of the bones and the joints. It's main functions are to provide support for the body, protect the internal organs, serve as a reservoir for certain minerals, and play a role in blood cell formation.

The skeletal muscles control an animal's movement, help maintain posture and alignment, and produce body heat. The body uses heat generated by muscles to maintain a constant internal temperature.

This chapter will present several illustrations and diagrams of the musculoskeletal system. For a more detailed description of the body parts and their functions, see *The Veterinary Assistant Career and Medical Terminology* (chapter 9, "Structure, Movement, and Support").

The Skeletal System

Bone is the second hardest substance in an animal's body—only tooth enamel is harder. Bone is also a vital, living tissue with an excellent capacity to repair itself after injury. Bones have a rich blood supply. Most bones have one nutrient artery and a vein. Bones also have a rich nerve supply, which is why pain is felt when bone injuries occur.

Animals vary greatly in the number of bones they have. For example, horses have just over 200 bones, but some dogs may have more than 300!

Bones are divided into five categories:

- Long, found in the limbs
- Short, found in the joints
- Sesamoid, found near joints, for example, the patella (knee cap)
- Flat, found in the skull, ribs, pelvis, and scapula
- Irregular, found in the vertebrae and some parts of the skull

Figure 3.1 Types of Bones

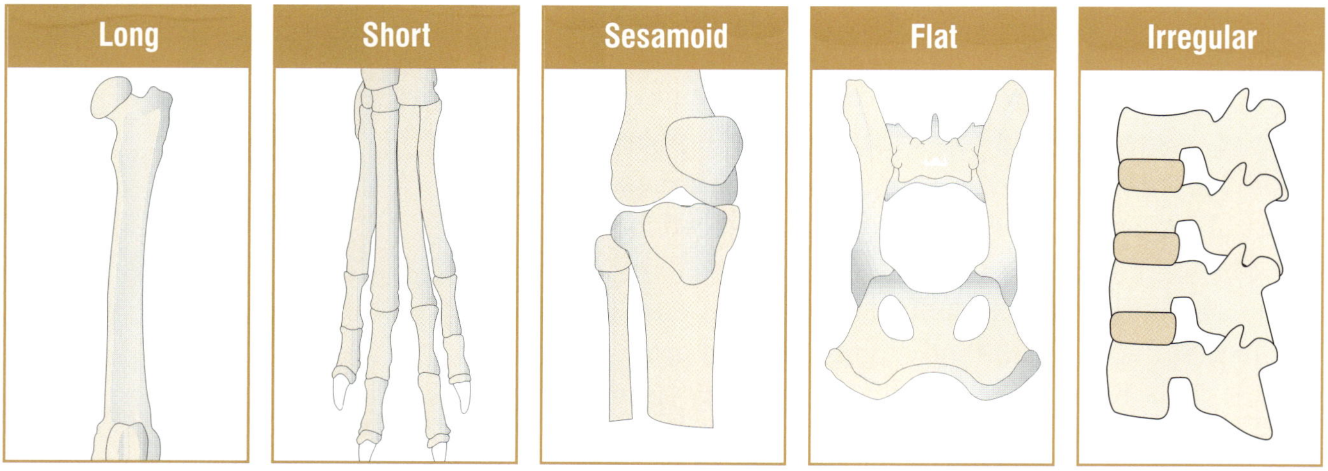

Long bones have cavities that contain two types of bone marrow:

- Yellow bone marrow stores fat.
- Red bone marrow produces blood cells.

Large blood vessels enter long bones to carry blood into and out of bone marrow, supplying blood with new blood cells. Short, irregular, and flat bones also contain bone marrow. But, unlike long bones, they have no bone marrow cavity.

There are two main parts of the skeleton:

- The axial skeleton comprises the bones of the head and trunk. These include the skull, vertebral column, ribs, and sternum (breast bone). The axial skeleton forms the central core to which the appendicular skeleton attaches.
- The appendicular skeleton includes the limbs (appendages) and makes motion possible. It comprises the forelimbs, hind limbs, scapula (shoulder blade), and pelvis.

The Axial Skeleton

The following sections illustrate the major bones in the axial skeleton.

The Skull

The skull has four main parts:

- The cranium
- The right and left mandibles
- The right and left maxilla
- The hyoid apparatus

Figure 3.2 Dog Skull

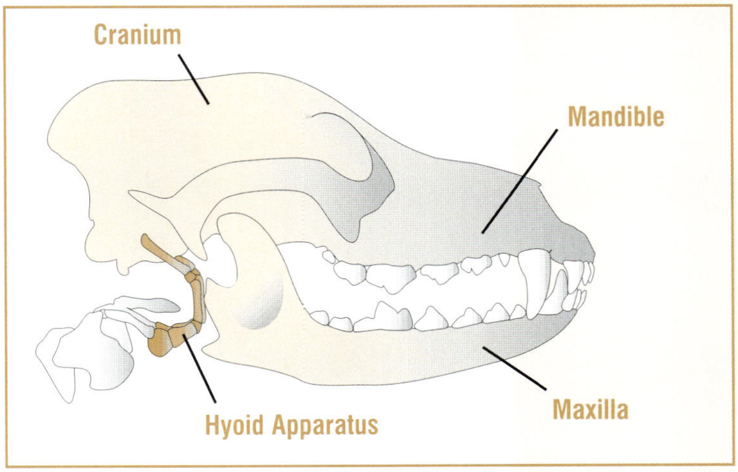

The main job of the skull is to protect the brain. It also supports the facial muscles and provides a channel for air to enter the body.

The Vertebral Column

The vertebral column is a series of irregular bones running from the base of the skull to the tip of the tail. It protects the spinal cord and provides support for many other body parts.

The vertebral column has five sections, each with a different number of vertebrae. The five sections are cervical (neck), thoracic (chest), lumbar (abdomen), sacral (pelvis), and coccygeal (tail). Table 3.1 lists the number of vertebrae found in domestic animals.

Figure 3.3 Vertebral Column

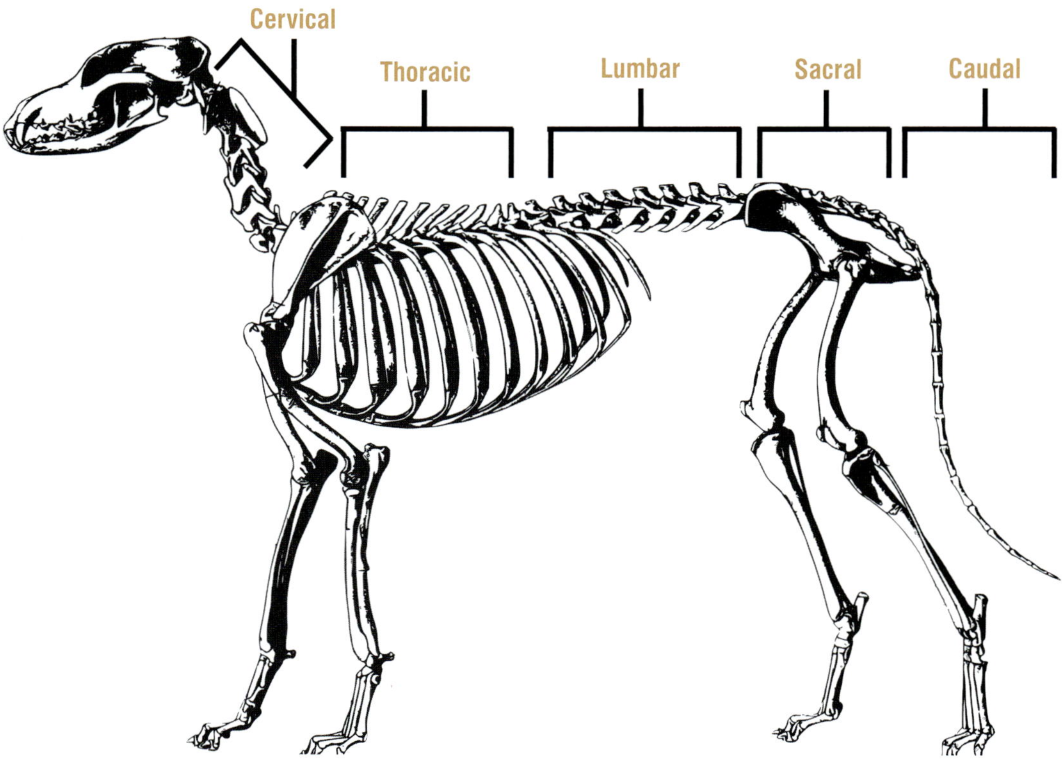

Species	Cervical	Thoracic	Lumbar	Sacral	Caudal (depends on tail length)
Dogs and cats	7	13	7	3	20–24
Pigs	7	11–15	6–7	4	20–23
Horses	7	18	6	5	15–21
Cattle	7	13	6	5	18–20
Sheep and goats	7	13	6–7	4	16–18

Table 3.1 Number of Vertebrae in Domestic Animals

The Rib Cage and Sternum

The thoracic cavity is formed by the rib cage, which protects the heart and lungs and enables respiration to occur.

The rib cage consists of three major parts:

- The ribs
- The sternum
- The thoracic vertebrae

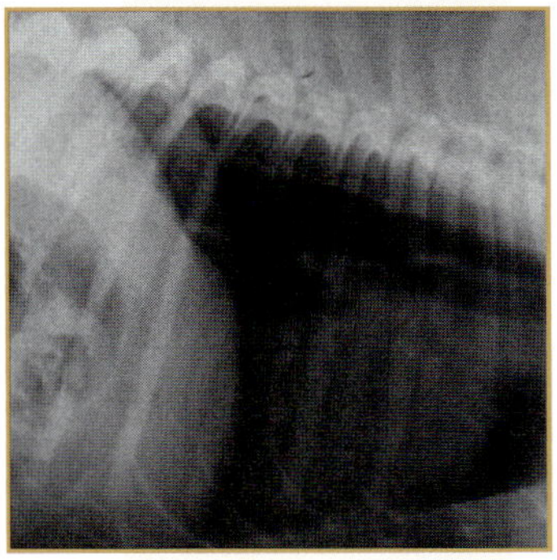

Figure 3.4 Rib Cage and Sternum

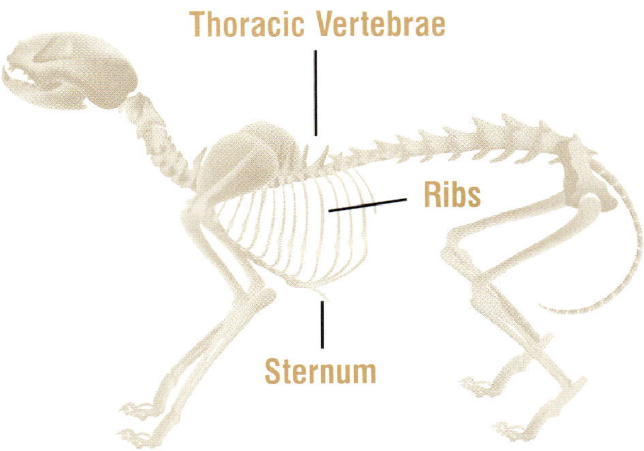

In dogs, cats, cattle, sheep, and goats, the ribs consist of 13 pairs of elongated flat bones, which form the walls of the cage. The horse has a longer rib cage with 18 ribs. Pigs have between 11 and 15.

The freely moveable joints between the heads of the ribs and the thoracic vertebrae help the movement of air in and out of the lungs.

The sternum is made up of several bones, called sternabrae, which are linked by joints made of cartilage. Dogs and cats have eight sternabrae; ruminants have seven; pigs and horses have six.

The Appendicular Skeleton

The following sections illustrate the major bones in the appendicular skeleton.

The Foreleg and Scapula

Figure 3.5 Bones of the Foreleg

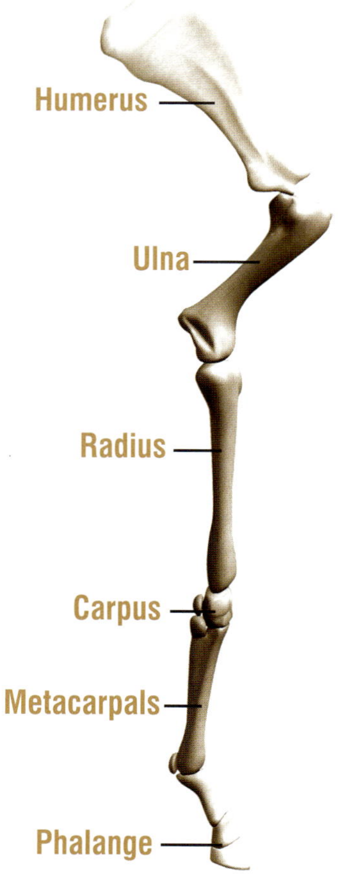

The scapula (shoulder blade) is attached to the spinal column by several muscles. It forms the shoulder joint with the humerus.

The major bones in the foreleg are as follows:

- The humerus
- The radius
- The ulna
- The carpus
- Metacarpals
- Phalanges

The number of metacarpals and phalanges varies by species. Pigs have four metacarpals, and ruminants have two. Horses have three metacarpals—a large metacarpal commonly referred to as the "cannon bone" and two smaller splint bones. Phalanges are an animal's toe bones. Most domestic animals have four main weight-bearing digits, or toes. Dogs and cats have a fifth, short toe, called a dew claw, which does not bear weight. Horses have one toe.

The Hind Leg and Pelvis

The pelvis forms the hip joint with the femur. The main regions of the pelvis are the ilium, the ischium, and the pubis. The ilium is the cranial-most bone of the pelvis. The ischium is the caudal-most bone, and the pubis is located medially.

The major bones in the hind leg are as follows:

- The femur
- The tibia
- The fibula
- The tarsus
- Metatarsals
- Phalanges

Figure 3.6 Bones of the Hind Leg

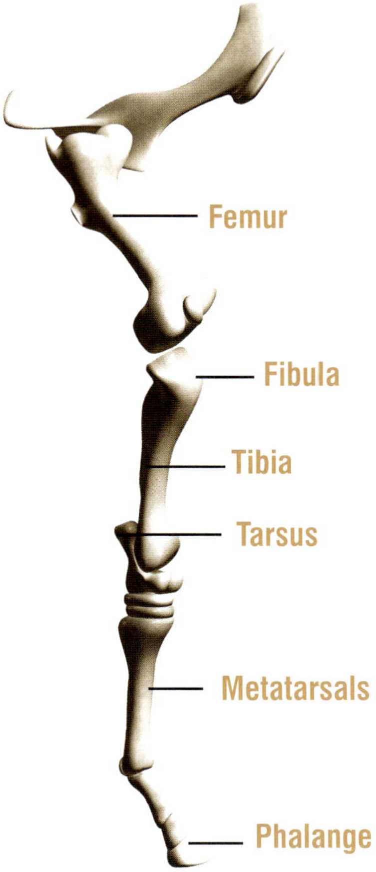

Like metacarpals, the number of metatarsals also varies by species. Cats, dogs, and pigs all have four metatarsals. Horses have three, and ruminants have two.

Figure 3.7 The Pelvis

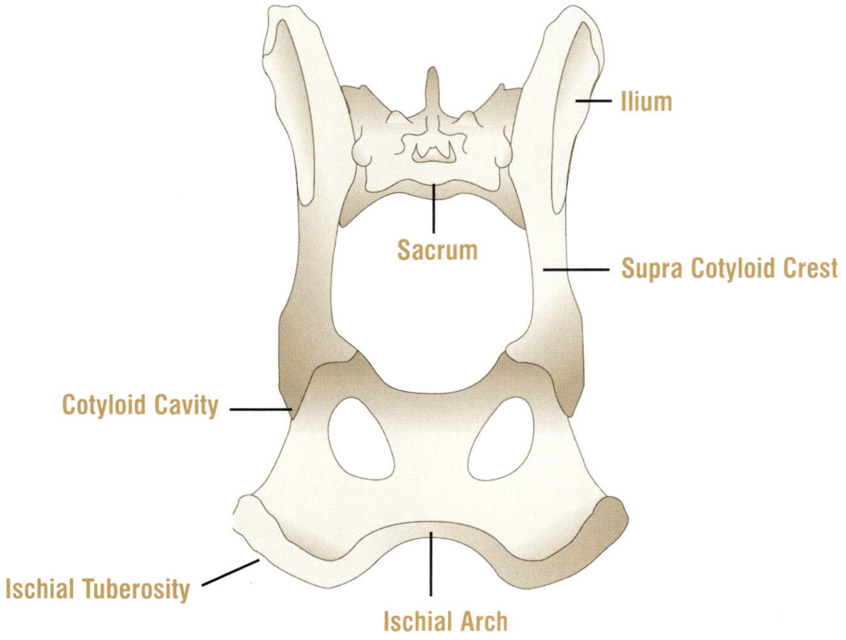

Figure 3.8 Skeleton of a Horse

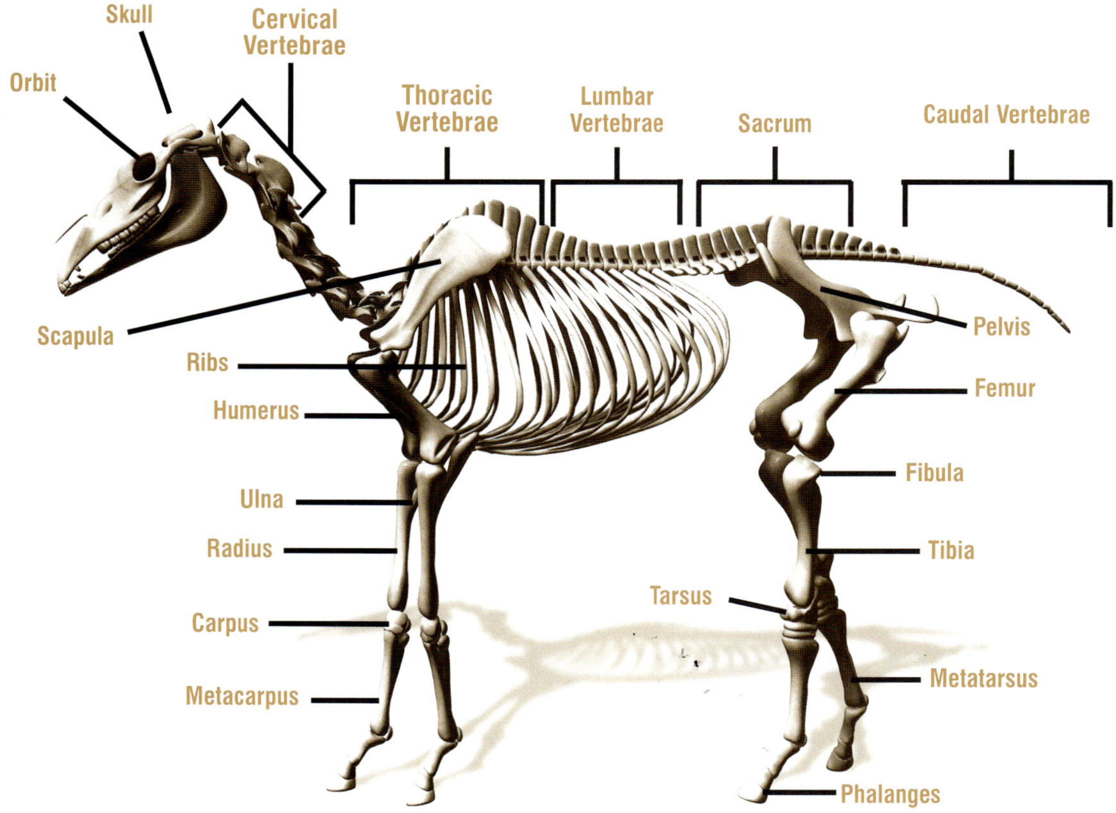

Table 3.2 Locations and Types of Bones

Bone	Location	Type of Bone
Skull	Head; protects the brain and supports the face	Flat or irregular
Cervical vertebrae	Neck	Irregular
Thoracic vertebrae	Chest	Irregular
Lumbar vertebrae	Abdomen	Irregular
Sacral vertebrae	Pelvic region	Irregular
Caudal vertebrae	Tail	Irregular
Pelvis	Pelvic region	Flat
Femur	Upper hind leg	Long
Fibula	Lower hind leg	Long
Tibia	Lower hind leg	Long
Tarsus	Ankle	Short
Metatarsus	Paw; between the heel and the phalanges	Short
Phalanges	Toes	Short
Metacarpus	Paw; in the foreleg between the carpus and the phalanges	Short
Carpus	Wrist	Short
Ulna	Lower foreleg	Long
Radius	Lower foreleg	Long
Humerus	Upper foreleg	Long
Ribs	Rib cage	Flat
Scapula	Shoulder bone	Flat
Lower maxillary	Lower jaw	Flat
Orbit	Cavity of the skull containing the eye	Flat

Joints

Joints are areas where two or more bones or cartilage are connected. They are strengthened by ligaments, which are dense connective tissues.

There are three main types of joints, classified according to the amount of movement they allow:

- Fibrous joints (immovable)
- Cartilaginous joints (slightly moveable)
- Synovial joints (freely moveable)

Synovial joints contain two or more bones. There are four different types of synovial joints:

- Hinge joints allow movement in only one plane.
- Ball-and-socket joints allow a wide range of movement.
- Pivot joints allow rotation.
- Gliding joints mainly allow flexion and extension.

For more information on the types of movement allowed by the different synovial joints, see Table 9.3 in *The Veterinary Assistant Career and Medical Terminology* (page 163).

Figure 3.9 Synovial Joints

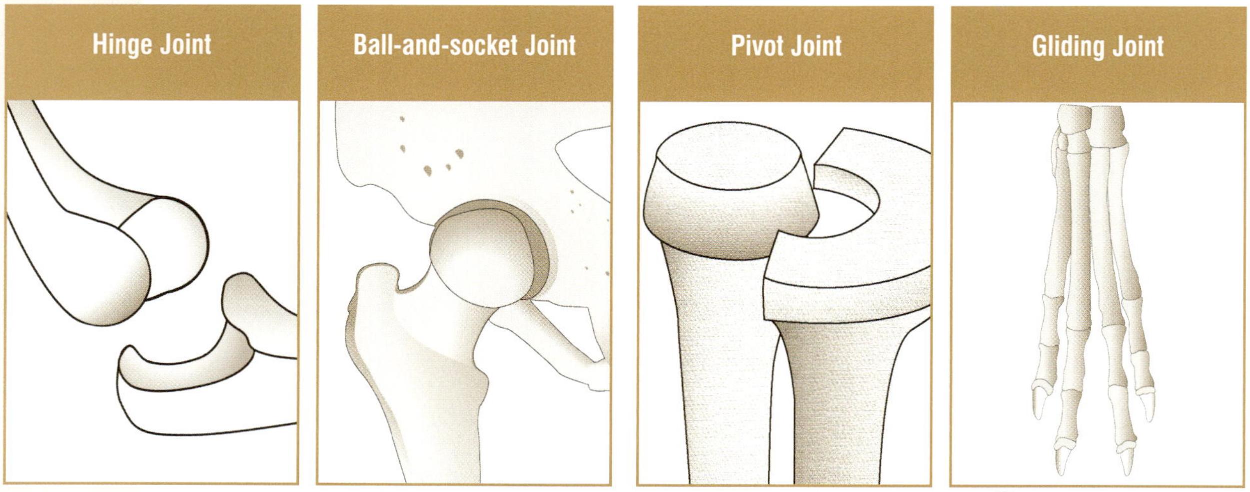

The Muscular System

The muscular system is composed of a specialized tissue containing cells that are capable of contracting. Muscles come in a variety of shapes and sizes, but they usually have a thick central portion called the belly and two or more attachment sites that join them to the tissues they move when they contract.

In addition to skeletal muscles and bones, an animal's musculoskeletal system also includes the following tissues and structures:

- Fascia binds muscle fibers together.
- Tendons attach muscles to bones.
- Ligaments connect bones together.
- Cartilage helps joints to move while absorbing some of the forces within them.
- Bursae act as cushions to relieve stress at certain joints.

Figure 3.10 Musculoskeletal Tissue

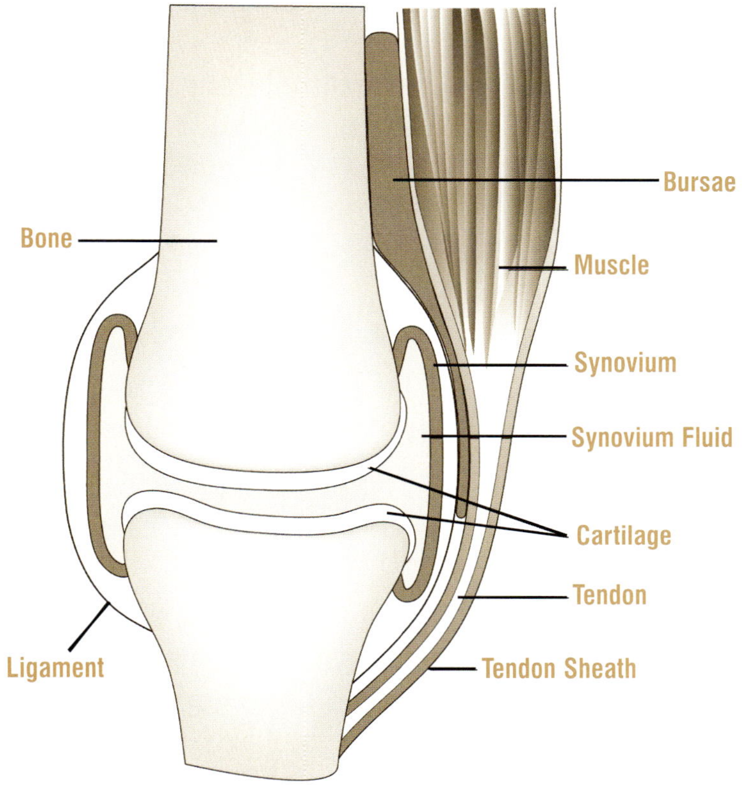

How Muscles Allow Movement

Muscles enable moving by contracting (shortening) and relaxing (lengthening). When a muscle contracts, it pulls on a tendon, which in turn pulls on a bone. When a muscle relaxes, it returns to its original position.

For joints to bend, muscles must work in pairs. A flexor muscle flexes the joint, and an extensor muscle extends the joint. Therefore, for a joint to bend, one muscle must contract and the other muscle must be relaxed.

Muscle Attachments

Muscles are attached to bones by tendons at both ends. One of a muscle's attachment sites is more stable and moves less than the other. This more stable site is called the origin of the muscle. It does not move much when the muscle contracts. The site that undergoes most of the movement when a muscle contracts is called the insertion of the muscle.

For example, the origin of the triceps brachii muscle, which is the muscle on the back of the upper arm, is on the scapula and humerus. Its insertion is on the point of the elbow, which is part of the ulna bone. When the triceps muscle contracts, it pulls on the point of the elbow and straightens, or extends, the elbow joint.

Muscle Anatomy

The following illustrations show the major muscles and muscle groups found in a domestic animal's head, trunk, chest, abdomen, and limbs.

The Head

The muscles of the head include the muscles responsible for facial expression as well as those responsible for chewing food and moving the tongue.

There are three muscles that operate the jaw:

- The masseter
- The temporal muscle
- The digastricus

Figure 3.9 Head Muscules

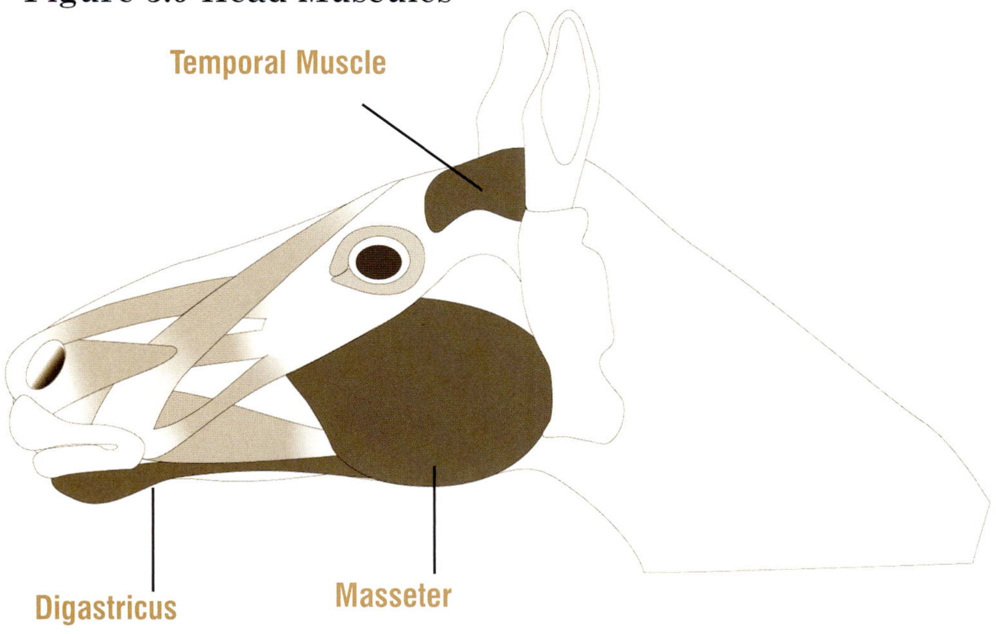

The Trunk

The muscles of the vertebral column are divided into epaxial muscles, attached to the pelvis, sacrum, ribs, and individual vertebrae, and hypaxial muscles, which lie ventral to the vertebrae.

Epaxial muscles perform several functions:

- Supporting the spine
- Helping animals to move
- Supporting the weight of the head, neck, and tail
- Allowing individual vertebrae to rotate somewhat

Hypaxial muscles help support the spine.

The Chest

There are three major muscle groups in the chest:

- Intercostal ("between ribs") muscles are necessary for respiration.
- The diaphragm allows the chest cavity to expand and contract during respiration.
- Superficial muscles protect both the ribs and the intercostal muscles.

Figure 3.11 Chest Muscles

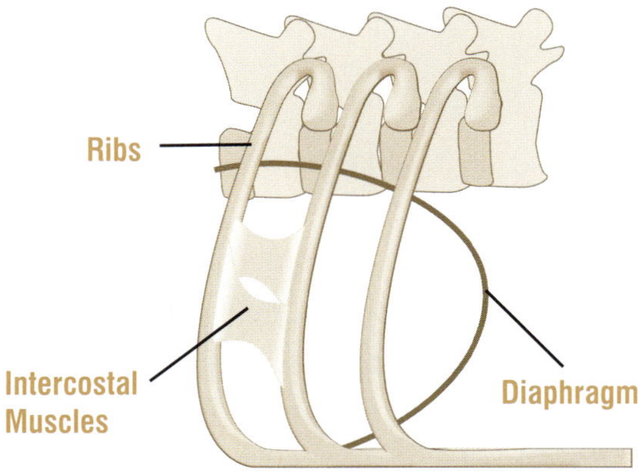

The Abdomen

There are four major abdominal muscles:

- The external abdominal oblique
- The internal abdominal oblique
- The transversus abdominis
- Rectus abdominis

Figure 3.12 Abdominal Muscles

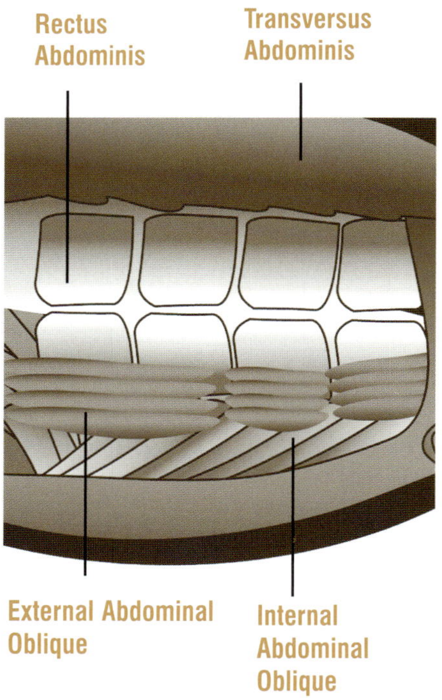

These muscles form the sides of the abdominal body wall and protect the soft tissues in the abdominal cavity. The muscle fibers run in all directions, which gives great strength to the abdomen. The oblique muscles are given that name because their fibers run in an oblique, or slanting, direction to the long axis of the body and opposite to each other.

Abdominal muscles also expel waste materials from the body and assist with the expiration of air. When abdominal muscles contract during expiration, they push the abdominal muscles up against the diaphragm. This pushes the diaphragm back into its full dome shape and decreases the size of the chest cavity.

The Foreleg

The muscles of the foreleg help the animal to walk and run.

The trapezius is a diamond-shaped muscle with four points extending to the neck, the two shoulders, and the middle of the back. The trapezius raises and lowers the shoulders. Both the trapezius and the brachiocephalicus work together to draw the foreleg forward. The deltoid is a triangular muscle that extends from the scapula to the humerus. It abducts and flexes the shoulder joint.

The biceps branchii and triceps branchii muscles are both located in the upper forelimb. They have opposite actions on the elbow joint. The biceps flexes, or bends, the elbow, whereas the triceps extends, or straightens, the elbow.

For a list of the major muscles and muscle groups found in an animal's foreleg, along with their location on the body and the actions for which they are responsible, see Table 9.4 in *The Veterinary Assistant Career and Medical Terminology* (pages 167–168).

Figure 3.12 Foreleg Muscles

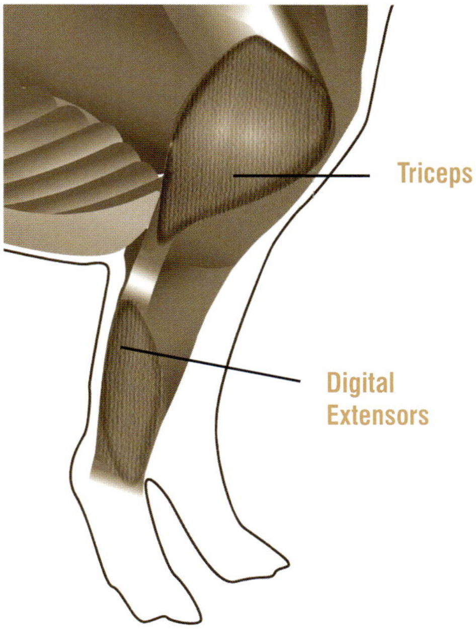

The Hind Leg

There are two major muscle groups in the hind leg: the hamstring group and the adductor group.

The hamstring group provides the propulsive force of the hind leg.

It includes three muscles:

- The biceps femoris
- The semitendinosus
- The semimembranosus

Figure 3.12 Hind Leg Muscles

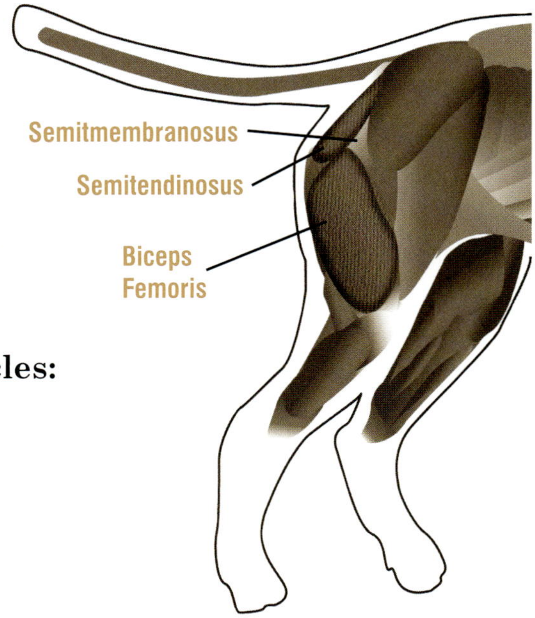

Muscles in the adductor group work to bring the limb toward the midline of the body.

There are four adductor muscles:

- The pectineus
- The adductor
- The gracilis
- The sartorius

Finally, located in the thigh region, the quadriceps femoris muscle is the main extensor muscle of the stifle joint. When an animal is walking or running, this muscle helps bring the leg forward to prepare for the next stride. As its name implies, this muscle has four heads, or attachments.

For a list of the major muscles and muscle groups found in an animal's foreleg, along with their location on the body and the actions for which they are responsible, see Table 9.5 in *The Veterinary Assistant Career and Medical Terminology* (pages 170–171).

Summary

The skeletal system consists of the bones forming the skeleton and the joints, which link the bones together. It has the following functions:

- Providing support for an animal's body
- Protecting delicate internal organs, including the brain, heart, and lungs
- Serving as a reservoir for such minerals as calcium and phosphorous
- Serving a function in blood cell formation

The skeleton has two parts: the axial skeleton that forms the head and trunk and the appendicular skeleton that makes motion possible.

A joint is where two or more bones or cartilage are connected. The three types of joints are fibrous joints that are immovable, cartilaginous joints that permit limited movement, and synovial joints that permit a wide range of movement. Synovial joints include the shoulder, hip, and knee.

The skeletal muscles of the muscular system determine and control an animal's movement, help maintain posture and alignment, and produce body heat by contracting. Muscles allow movement through contraction and relaxation. Contraction occurs when the muscle shortens to pull on a bone. Relaxation occurs when the muscle lengthens to return to its original position.

Key Terms

Term	Definition
Appendicular skeleton	The part of the skeleton that makes motion possible and protects the organs of digestion, excretion, and reproduction. It comprises the limbs, shoulders, and pelvis.
Axial skeleton	The bones of the head and trunk in the body, including the skull, vertebral column, ribs, and sternum. The axial skeleton protects the brain, heart, and lungs.
Bone marrow	Flexible tissue found in the hollow interior of long bones that stores fat (yellow bone marrow) and produces blood cells (red bone marrow).
Bursae	Small fluid sacs found at the friction points around joints that cushion them from stress.
Cartilage	A more rigid form of connective tissue found in joints between bones.
Cartilaginous joint	A joint that permits only limited movement, such as compression or stretching. Cartilaginous joints are found in the sternabrae (bones in the sternum) and vertebrae (bones in the vertebral column).
Compact bone	The material that forms the hard outer surface of bones.
Contraction	Occurs when a muscle shortens to pull on a bone.
Fascia	Connective tissue that covers and binds muscle fibers together.
Fibrous joint	Immovable joint found at sites where the surfaces of bones are in almost direct contact, separated only by connective tissue. Examples include sutures between the different bones of the skull and the joints between teeth and the mandible and maxilla of the skull.

Key Terms

Term	Definition
Fibrocartilage	A specialized type of cartilage that contains both fibrous connective tissue and cartilage.
Flat bone	Flat, thin, and sometimes curved bone found in the skull, ribs, scapula, and pelvis.
Irregular bones	Bones of various shapes that do not fit into the other categories. Irregular bones are found in the vertebrae of the spine and some parts of the skull.
Ligament	A strong, flexible band of connective tissue that connects bone to bone and provides support to joints.
Long bone	Bone that is longer than it is wide, which has a shaft and two ends. Long bones are found in the limbs and contain bone marrow.
Muscular system	The body system consisting of the skeletal muscles that contract to control movement, smooth muscle found in internal organs, and cardiac muscle found in the heart.
Musculoskeletal system	The body system that makes movement possible. It is divided into the skeletal and muscular systems.
Relaxation	Occurs when a muscle lengthens to return to its original position.
Sesamoid bones	Bones that resemble sesame seeds and are found near joints.
Short bone	Cube-shaped bone found in the joints, such as the wrist and ankle.
Skeletal system	The system that consists of the bones forming the skeleton and the joints, which link the bones together.

Key Terms

Term	Definition
Spongy bone	Low-density bone tissue that forms the inside of bones and houses bone marrow.
Synovial joint	Joint that allows various types of movement and contains two or more bones. The four different types of synovial joints are hinge, ball-and-socket, pivot, and gliding.
Tendon	Dense connective tissue that attaches muscles to bones and helps with movement.

What Do You Remember?

Answer key on page 199

Exercise 3–1

1. The tibia is a/an ________ bone.

a. long
b. short
c. irregular
d. flat

2. The tarsus is a/an ________ bone.

a. long
b. short
c. irregular
d. flat

3. The scapula is a/an ________ bone.

a. long
b. short
c. irregular
d. flat

4. The ________ is an example of a gliding joint.

a. shoulder
b. hip
c. wrist
d. knee

5. The ________ is an example of a hinge joint.

a. shoulder
b. hip
c. wrist
d. knee

Answer key on page 199

What Do You Remember?

6. ___________ **attach skeletal muscles to bones.**

a. Tendons
b. Ligaments
c. Cartilage
d. Fascia

7. ___________ **attach bone to bone at joints.**

a. Tendons
b. Ligaments
c. Cartilage
d. Fascia

Exercise 3–2

Match the five sections of vertebrae with their location on the spinal column.

1. cervical	a. tail
2. sacral	b. neck
3. caudal	c. chest
4. thoracic	d. abdomen
5. lumbar	e. pelvis

Answer key on page 199

What Do You Remember?

Exercise 3–3

Match the following bones with their location in the body.

1. femur
2. fibula
3. tarsus
4. phalanges
5. humerus
6. radius
7. scapula
8. sternum
9. metacarpus
10. metatarsus

a. front paw
b. upper hind leg
c. lower foreleg
d. shoulder
e. underside of the rib cage
f. hind paw
g. lower hind leg
h. upper foreleg
i. ankle
j. toes

Brown Labrador Retriever

CHAPTER 4

The Cardiovascular System and the Blood

Highlights of the Chapter

- The structure and function of the heart and blood systems
- Heart contractions and the cardiac cycle
- Key terms related to the heart
- The components of blood
- Blood and the diagnosis of disease
- Venipuncture sites

Introduction

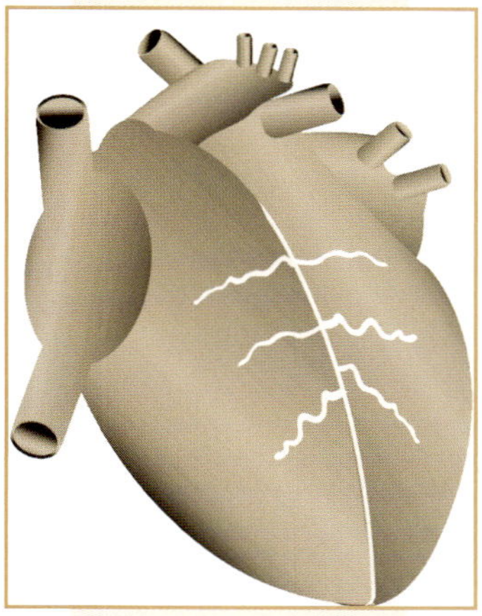

The cardiovascular system is made up of the heart and the blood vessels. Its job is to carry blood to tissues and cells throughout the body.

Blood is a living tissue. It is responsible for transporting nutrients, oxygen, and water to cells, as well as removing carbon dioxide and other waste products from cells. In order to survive, all cells in an animal's body need a continuous supply of oxygen and continuous removal of carbon dioxide.

This chapter will provide an overview of the cardiovascular system. For more details on the system and its components, see *The Veterinary Assistant Career and Medical Terminology* (chapter 7, "Essential Life Support").

The Cardiovascular System

The main organ of the cardiovascular system is the heart, which is located in the ventral chest cavity.

In addition, there are five major types of blood vessels:

- Arteries
- Arterioles
- Capillaries
- Veins
- Venules

Arteries, arterioles, and capillaries transport oxygenated blood to the various tissues throughout the body. The aorta, which is the largest artery in the body, is connected to the heart. Venules carry deoxygenated blood back from the various tissues in the body.

The Heart

The heart is composed of cardiac muscle, an involuntary muscle tissue which is found only within this organ. The heart is divided into four chambers: two upper atria, and two lower ventricles. The heart is divided into right and left sides by a muscular wall called the septum.

Figure 4.1 The Heart Chambers

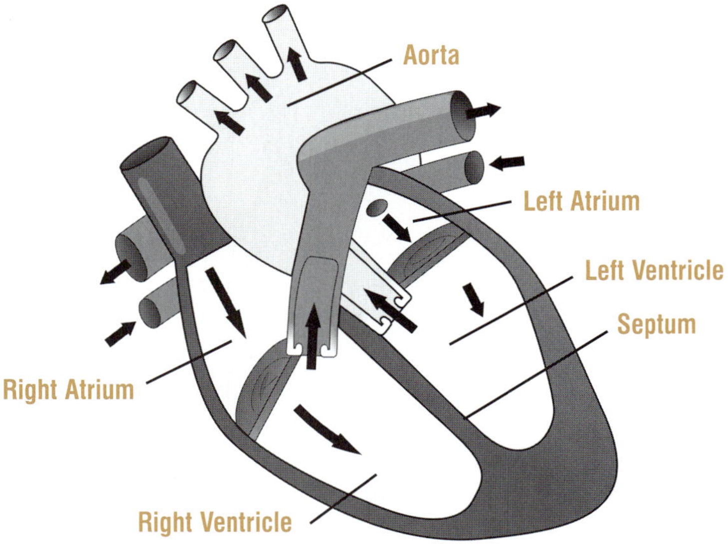

The membrane surrounding the heart is the pericardium. The pericardium anchors the heart in place and keeps it from overfilling with blood.

The heart muscle has three layers:

- The epicardium
- The myocardium
- The endocardium

Figure 4.2 The Heart

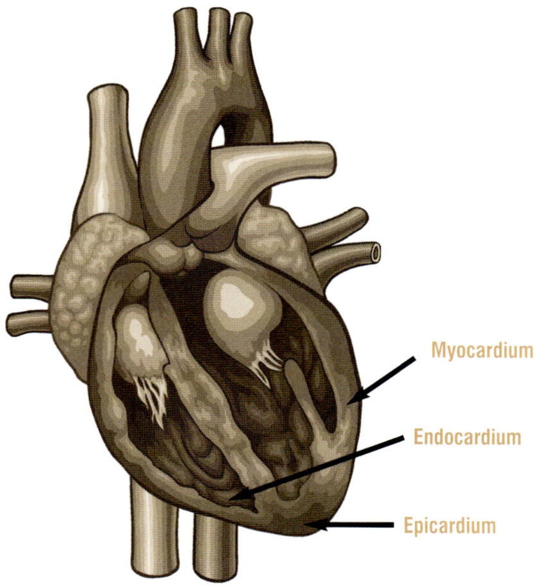

There are two types of blood circulation:

- Pulmonary circulation is the movement of blood between the heart and the lungs.
- Systemic circulation is the movement of blood between the heart and the rest of the body.

The following figure shows the process of circulation.

Figure 4.3 Pulmonary and Systemic Circulation

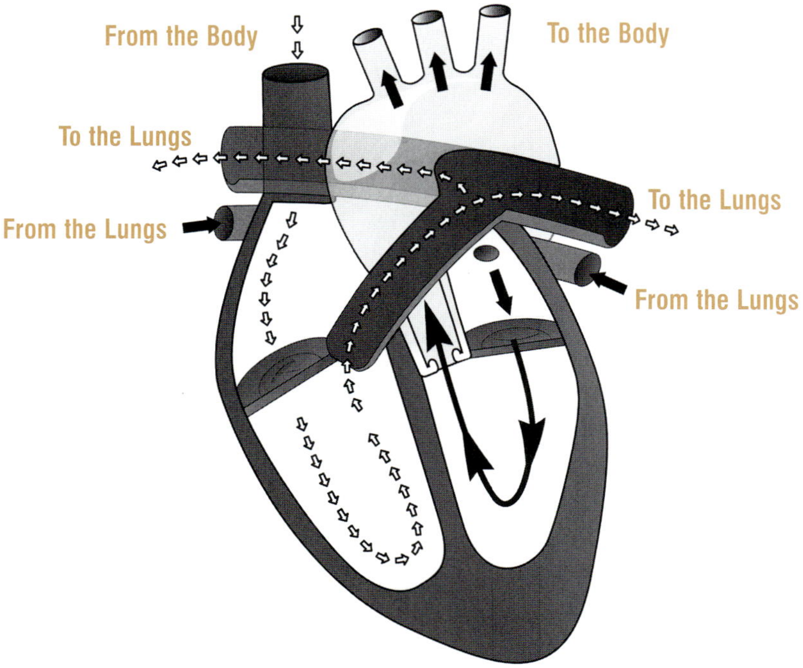

Deoxygenated blood enters the right atrium of the heart and flows into the right ventricle, where it is pumped through the pulmonary artery to the lungs. In the lungs, the blood is oxygenated, which means that the waste-filled blood is exchanged for oxygen-rich blood. The oxygenated blood returns to the heart via the pulmonary vein. It enters the left atrium and flows into the left ventricle. The oxygen-rich blood is then pumped out to the rest of the body via the aorta.

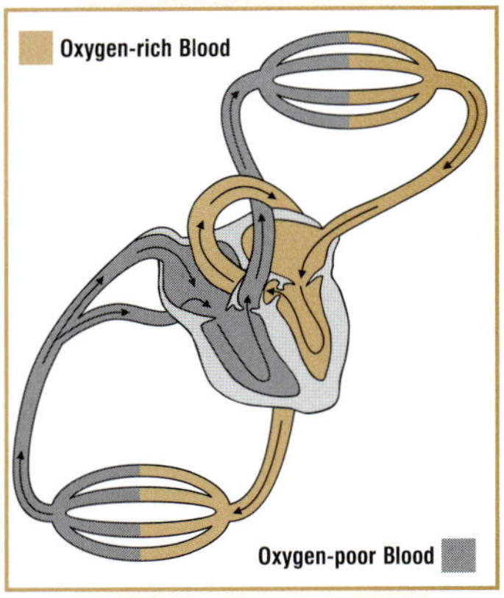

Heart valves maintain the unidirectional flow of blood in the heart by opening and closing depending on the difference in pressure on each side.

There are four main heart valves:

- The two atrioventricular (AV) valves are between the atria and the ventricles. The left AV valve is called the mitral valve. The right AV valve is called the tricuspid valve.
- The two semilunar (SL) valves are in the arteries leaving the heart. The SL valves are the aortic and pulmonary valves, which control blood flow to the aorta and pulmonary arteries.

The blood travels through various arterial branches to the capillaries, where oxygen and nutrient exchange take place. After passing through tissue capillaries, deoxygenated blood travels back to the heart through progressively larger venules and veins until it once again passes through the coronary veins into the right atrium.

Heart Contractions and the Cardiac Cycle

Special cells in the heart's right atrium generate electrical impulses. This tissue acts as the heart's pacemaker. The electrical impulses travel through the heart muscle, stimulating muscle fibers to contract.

Each complete contraction and relaxation of the heart, or heart beat, is called the "cardiac cycle." The two main parts of the cardiac cycle are systole and diastole. During systole, the heart muscle contracts to pump blood from the atria to the ventricles and then from the ventricles to the arteries. During diastole, the heart relaxes and refills with blood to be ejected during the next contraction.

The cardiac cycle has three major stages:

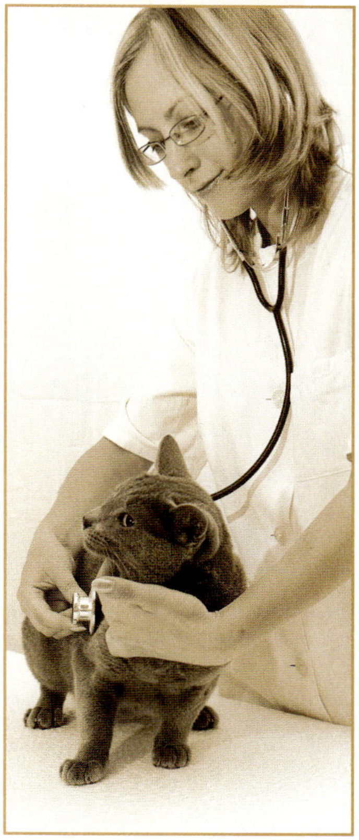

1. *Atrial systole.* The right and left atria contract simultaneously, while the ventricles remain relaxed. The blood pressure in the atria increases, forcing blood into the ventricles. About 70% of the blood flows passively down to the ventricles, so the atria do not have to contract a great amount.
2. *Ventricular systole.* The atria relax, and the ventricles contract. At this stage, the blood pressure in the ventricles becomes much higher than the pressure in both the atria and the arteries. This causes the AV valves to snap shut and forces the SL valves to the arteries to open. The right ventricle pumps deoxygenated blood into the pulmonary artery for transport to the lungs. The left ventricle pushes oxygenated blood into the aorta for transportation to body tissues by smaller blood vessels.
3. *Cardiac diastole.* During this stage, the heart relaxes after contracting, in preparation for refilling with circulating blood. Ventricular diastole occurs when the ventricles are relaxing; atrial diastole occurs when the atria are relaxing. Together, they are known as "complete cardiac diastole."

As the pressure in the ventricles decreases, blood in the aorta and pulmonary arteries begins to return to the heart and the SL valves close. The atria fill with blood, and pressure in the ventricles falls below the pressure of the atria. This pulls the AV valves open in preparation for atrial systole.

Normal Heart Sounds

In all species, the heart is auscultated, or listened to, through the chest wall, usually with a stethoscope. Two clearly audible sounds are created during each heart beat. These sounds are typically described as "lub-dup." The first sound, "lub," is the AV valves closing as blood begins returning to the atria at the beginning of

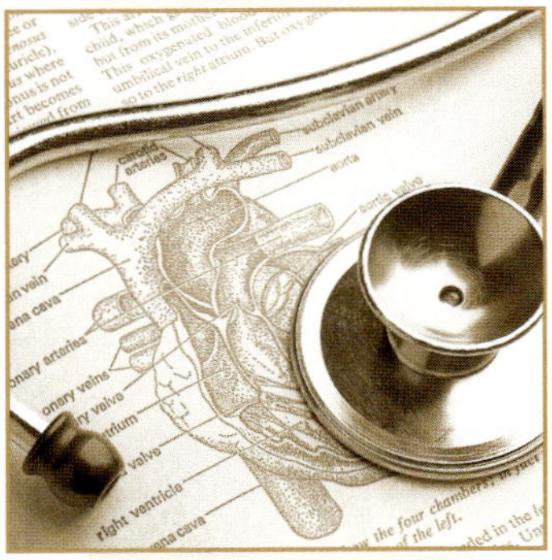

ventricular systole. This sound is louder and longer than the second sound. The "dup" sound is caused by the SL valves closing at the beginning of ventricular diastole.

Due to the orientation of the heart in the chest, the mitral valve is loudest on the left side of the chest, whereas the tricuspid valve is best heard on the right. Both SL valves are easiest to hear on the left side of the chest.

Key Terms Related to the Heart

Blood Pressure

Blood pressure is the pressure placed on the walls of the heart and blood vessels as blood circulates through the body. Blood pressure readings are recorded as a ratio of two numbers. The top number represents "systole," which is the pressure in the vessels as the heart is contracting. The bottom number is "diastole," the pressure in the vessels when the heart is at rest between contractions.

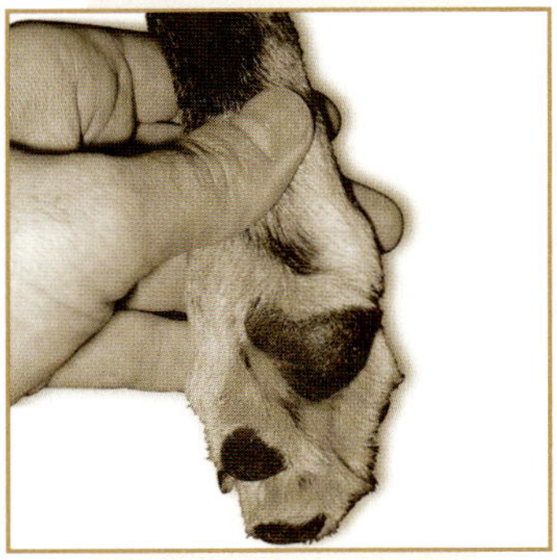

Pulse

The term *pulse* refers to how often the heart contracts, or the heart rate. Pulses are felt because of the pressure differences during systole and diastole.

An animal's pulse is taken where an artery runs close to the body surface. The most common site used to take an animal's pulse is the femoral artery, located on the inside of the thigh in the groin region.

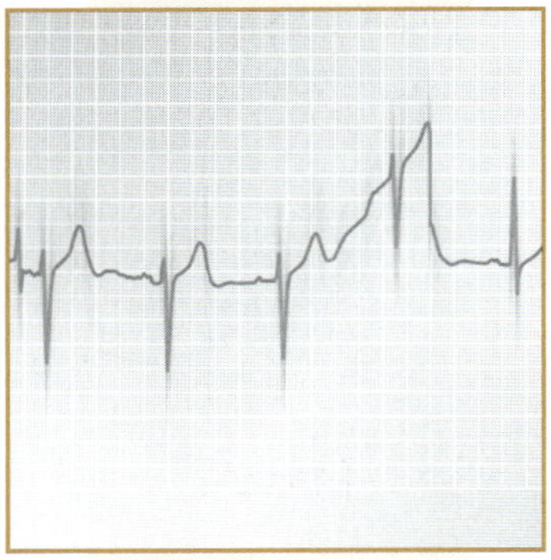

Other sites that can be used to take the pulse include the following:

- The coccygeal artery on the underside of the base of the tail
- The digital artery in the hind limb, located at the back of the paw between the carpal (upper) pad and the metacarpal (lower) pad

When an animal goes into shock, its blood pressure drops substantially and its pulse often becomes rapid and weak. Shock may be caused by blood loss, a severe allergic reaction, or infection.

During shock, less blood is pumped with each cardiac contraction. Increases in arterial blood pressure during systole are reduced, making the pulse weaker. At the same time, the heart rate increases to help compensate for the reduced amount of blood flow.

Conversely, during the fight-or-flight response to a perceived threat, the nervous system releases adrenaline, which increases the strength of the heart's contractions and the heart rate. This prepares the body for the increased cardiac output that will be needed to either flee or fight the threat.

Cardiac Output

Cardiac output is the volume of blood pumped out by the heart per minute.

It is determined by two factors:

- Stroke volume, which is the amount of blood pumped during each contraction
- The pulse or number of times the heart contracts

The relationship between cardiac output, heart rate, and stroke volume is shown in the following equation:

CO (Cardiac Output) = SV (Stroke Volume) X HR (Heart Rate)

So, if a dog's heart ejects 2 milliliters of blood into the aorta with each contraction, and its heart rate is 100 beats per minute, the animal's cardiac output is calculated as follows:

CO = 2 ml/minute (SV) X 100 beats/minute (HR) = 200 ml

The dog's cardiac output is 200 milliliters of blood per minute.

Various factors will affect an animal's cardiac output. For example, vigorous exercise increases the body's demand for oxygen. To meet the demand, the heart contracts more forcefully, which increases stroke volume. The heart also contracts more often, increasing the pulse. As the heart rate and stroke volume increase during exercise, cardiac output will also rise.

	Blood Pressure:	Pulse:
Human	120/80	72
Dog	133/75	60–180
Cat	124/84	120–240
Horse	120/70	30–45
Cattle	105/60	60–80

*Average Values

Congestive Heart Failure (CHF)

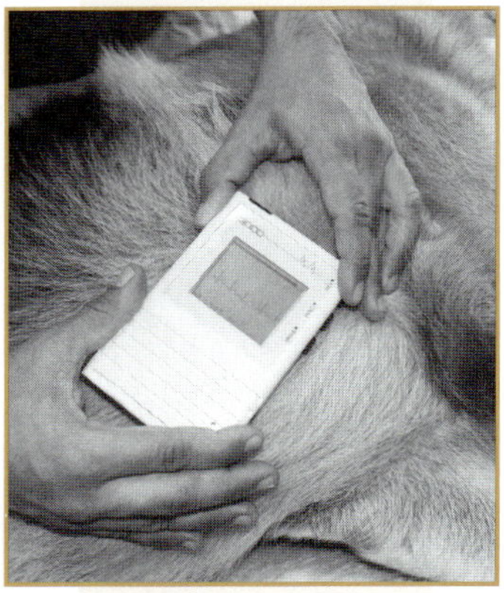

Congestive heart failure (CHF) is a common health problem in older dogs. It occurs when the heart's pumping ability decreases, due either to heart disease or to a valve malfunction that affects the forward flow of blood. Medications can be prescribed for animals with CHF to increase the strength of cardiac contractions, improve blood flow to organs, and decrease resistance to outflow from the heart. CHF in pets cannot be cured, but it can be medically managed to improve the animal's quality of life.

Electrocardiograms

Because cardiac contractions are the result of electrical currents, a machine that detects electrical currents is used to measure the heart's activity. This machine is called an electrocardiograph, which produces a chart on graph paper called an electrocardiogram (ECG). Electrical currents cause the stylus to move up and down on the paper, creating waves. Heart rate can be calculated by counting how often the waves occur.

Healthy hearts will produce a normal wave pattern, which is easy to identify on an ECG. By measuring the height and width of abnormal waves, heart abnormalities can be found.

The Blood System

The Components of Blood

Blood is made of plasma and blood cells. About 55% of blood is plasma, a yellow liquid that is mostly water (91.5%) and contains a variety of dissolved substances, such as electrolytes, proteins, glucose, and fats.The other 45% of blood is made of blood cells.

There are three types of blood cells:

- Erythrocytes (red blood cells)
- Leukocytes (white blood cells)
- Thrombocytes (platelets)

The three types of blood cells are formed in the bone marrow. In general, only the more mature cells are found in an animal's bloodstream. Since blood cells are continuously dying from old age or damage, they must constantly be replaced. For an animal to

remain healthy, it always needs a sufficient number of all of its blood cells.

In a newborn animal, red bone marrow is found in nearly all bones because there is a great demand for blood cells as the animal grows and matures. When an animal reaches adulthood, its need for blood cells decreases and some of the red bone marrow is converted to inactive yellow bone marrow that stores fat. In a mature animal, most of the red bone marrow is found at ends of long bones and flat bones. The rest of the skeleton contains yellow bone marrow.

Figure 4.1 Centrifuged Blood Sample

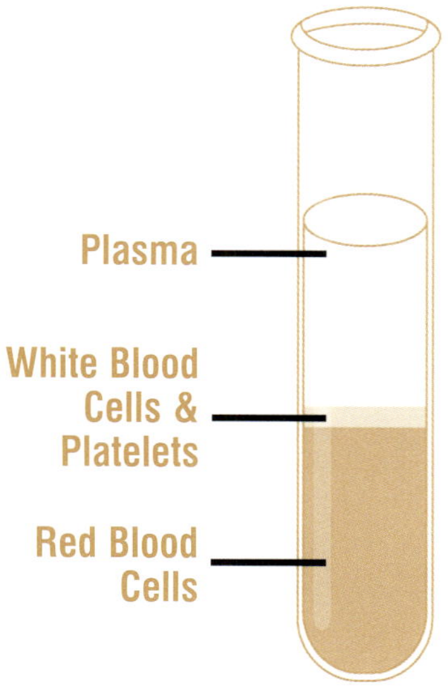

Figure 4.2 The Components of Blood

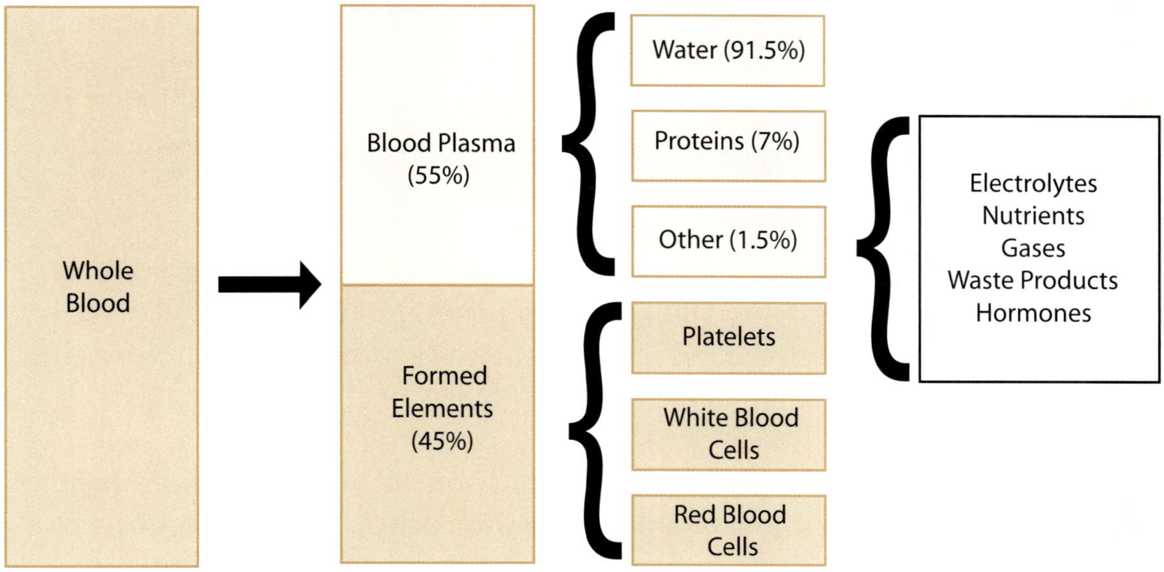

The Functions of Blood

Blood has three main functions: transportation, regulation, and defense. In order for the cells of an animal's body to perform their normal functions, they require a steady supply of oxygen, nutrients, and essential chemicals. Blood carries these three things to the body's cells, acting as a transport system. It also carries waste products such as carbon dioxide away from cells to the organs that excrete them from the body—the lungs and the kidneys. Finally, it transports hormones from endocrine glands to the tissues where they will do their work.

The blood's regulatory function includes helping to maintain a normal body temperature. In all mammals, skin blood flow is a critical component of temperature regulation. To dissipate heat, warm-blooded animals direct blood flow to the skin so the heat can be transferred to the surrounding environment. Skin capillaries dilate, or open, so that blood flows close to the skin.

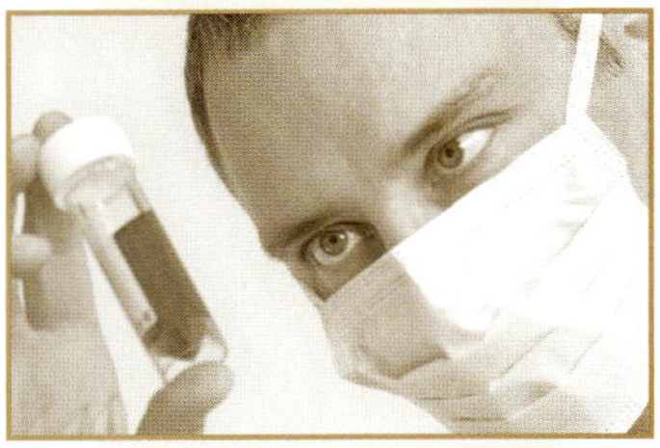

To warm up in cold temperatures, warm-blooded animals direct blood away from the skin. Skin capillaries constrict, or get smaller, so that blood flow moves away from the skin's surface. This helps to conserve heat and prevents its dissipation to the environment.

The blood system also helps to maintain normal levels of hydration and blood pH (the acid-base balance in the body). If an animal is dehydrated, plasma, which is 91.5% water, will leave the bloodstream and enter body tissues to compensate for fluid loss. If an animal is over-hydrated, the excess fluid will enter the bloodstream to help maintain homeostasis.

Blood acts as a defense system by using white blood cells to ingest foreign invaders into the body and boost immunity. Platelets and the clotting factors found in blood act quickly to stop bleeding when a blood vessel is damaged.

White blood cells travel from their site of production (the bone marrow) to their site of activity (body tissues). There is a constant flow of white blood cells from the marrow into tissues to control the millions of foreign invaders that attempt to attack the body. If an animal's white blood cells are functioning properly, it has a good chance of staying healthy.

Blood and the Diagnosis of Disease

The blood is an important tool for diagnosing disease in animals. Many diagnostic blood tests are done using a sample of either blood plasma or serum. Plasma is whole blood minus the cells. Serum is whole blood minus the cells and clotting elements. To produce plasma for a blood test, an anticoagulant is added to the sample to prevent it from clotting. The sample is then spun at high speed in a centrifuge. The fluid that rises to the top is plasma. The red blood cells sink to the bottom of the tube. The white blood cells, which are less dense and heavy, fall to the middle.

If no anticoagulant is added to a blood sample, the blood will clot. When clotted blood is centrifuged, the fluid that rises to the top of the tube is serum. The blood cells and clotting elements will separate from the serum.

After a blood sample has been centrifuged, the plasma or serum can be drawn off and analyzed or frozen for analysis at a later date.

Venipuncture Sites

Although most blood vessels are buried deep within the body, some are superficial and can be seen or felt under the skin. It is these superficial blood vessels that are used to collect blood samples, administer medications intravenously, and place intravenous catheters. The process of puncturing a vein with a needle is called venipuncture.

Blood vessels used for venipuncture include the following:

- The cephalic vein runs between the elbow and carpus in the medial aspect of the foreleg.
- The femoral vein runs along the medial aspect of the hind leg between the groin and the ankle joint.
- The saphenous vein runs along the lateral aspect of the hind limb, from just below the knee to just above the ankle.
- Jugular veins travel along both sides of the neck, from the lower jaw to the shoulder.
- The coccygeal, or tail, vein runs along the midline of the base of the tail.

The cephalic vein is commonly used for venipuncture in both dogs and cats. The femoral vein is more commonly used in cats; the saphenous vein is more commonly used in dogs. The coccygeal vein is often used for venipuncture in ruminants (cattle, sheep, and goats) and rodents (mice, rats, hamsters, gerbils, and guinea pigs). The jugular vein may be used for venipuncture in most animals, both large and small.

Figure 4.3 Commonly Used Venipuncture Sites

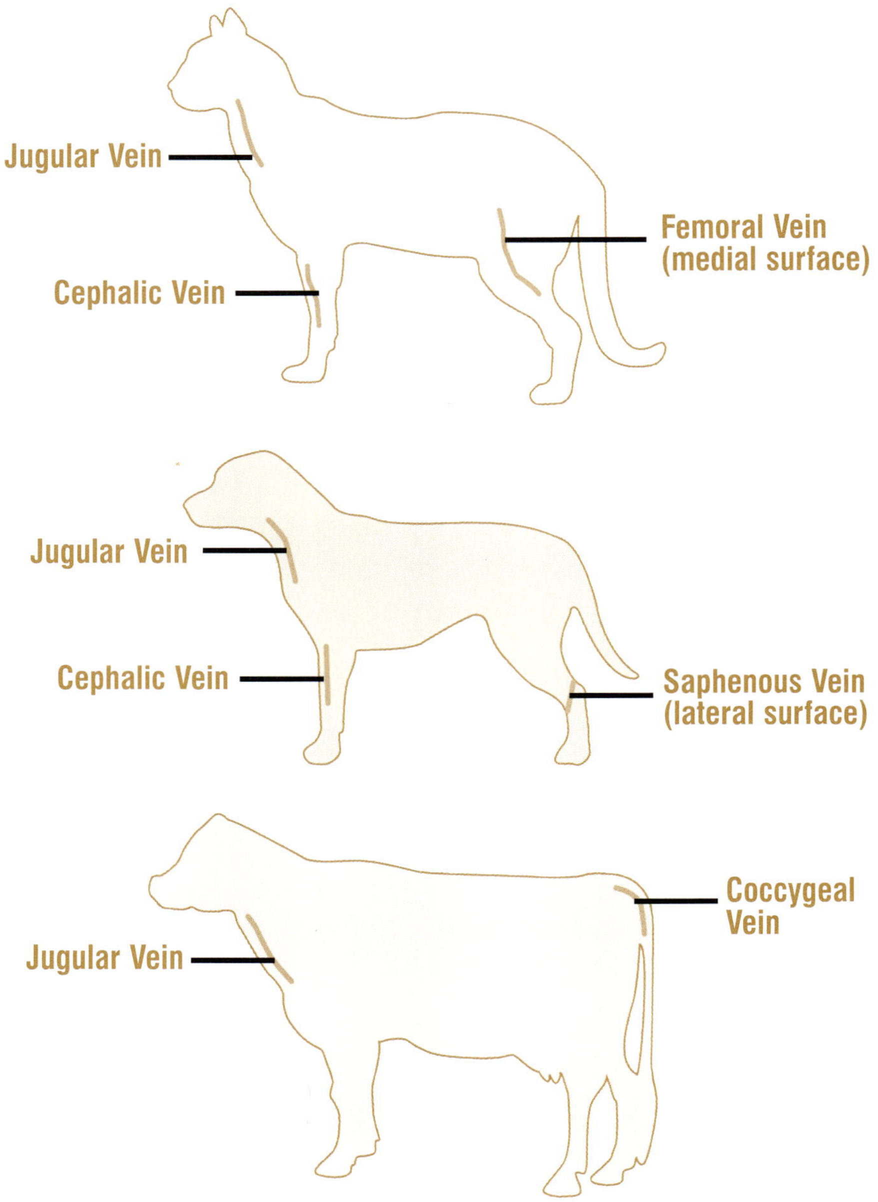

Summary

The cardiovascular system carries blood between the heart and various tissues and cells throughout the body. It consists of the heart and the blood vessels, which include arteries, veins, and capillaries.

Each complete contraction and relaxation of the heart, or heart beat, is called the "cardiac cycle." The two main parts of the cardiac cycle are systole and diastole. During systole, the heart muscle contracts to pump blood from the atria to the ventricles and then from the ventricles to the arteries. During diastole, the heart relaxes and refills with blood to be ejected during the next contraction.

Blood is the major transport medium of an animal's body. It provides a steady supply of oxygen, nutrients, and essential chemicals to cells.

Arteries, veins, and capillaries are all blood vessels. Arteries carry oxygenated blood away from the heart to the rest of the body, while veins carry deoxygenated blood back to the heart.

Movement of blood through blood vessels throughout the body is called circulation. Pulmonary circulation is the circulation between the heart and the lungs. Systemic circulation is the circulation of blood between the heart and the rest of the body.

Blood contains plasma and blood cells. The three types of blood cells are erythrocytes that deliver oxygen to body tissues, leukocytes that defend the body against infectious disease, and platelets that clot blood when wounds occur.

Key Terms

Term	Definition
Anticoagulant	A substance that stops blood from clotting.
Aorta	The largest artery in the body, originating from the left ventricle of the heart and bringing oxygenated blood to all parts of the body.
Atria	The upper chambers of the heart. There is a right and a left atrium.
Atrioventricular valves	The two heart valves that prevent backflow of blood from the ventricles into the atria during systole. The mitral valve controls blood flow between the left atrium and the left ventricle. The tricuspid valve controls blood flow between the right atrium and the right ventricle.
Blood	The major transport medium of an animal's body, carrying nutrients, oxygen, and water to cells and removing waste from them.
Blood pressure	The pressure placed on the walls of the heart and blood vessels as blood circulates through the body.
Bloodstream	The flowing blood in the cardiovascular system.
Cardiac output	The volume of blood pumped by the heart per minute.
Cardiovascular system	The body system comprising the heart and the blood vessels.
Circulation	The movement of blood through blood vessels throughout the body.
Congestive heart failure	A condition caused by heart disease in which the heart's ability to provide sufficient blood flow to meet the body's needs is impaired.
Diastole	The pressure in blood vessels when the heart is at rest between contractions.

Key Terms

Term	Definition
Electrocardiogram (ECG)	The printout of the electrical activity of the heart produced by an electrocardiograph.
Electrocardiograph	A machine that records the electrical activity of the heart via skin electrodes. It is often used to measure and diagnose abnormal heart rhythms.
Erythrocytes	Red blood cells that deliver oxygen to body tissues and remove carbon dioxide from them via the bloodstream.
Leukocytes	White blood cells that defend the body against infectious disease, allergies, and harmful bacteria.
Plasma	The yellow liquid in blood that contains dissolved substances, such as electrolytes, proteins, glucose, and fats. About 55% of blood is plasma.
Pulmonary circulation	The circulation of blood between the heart and the lungs.
Pulse	The heart rate, measured in beats per minute by palpating an artery.
Semilunar valves	The heart valves that control blood flow between the heart and the aorta and pulmonary artery, called the aortic and pulmonary valves.
Serum	Blood plasma with the clotting factors removed.
Stroke output	The amount of blood that leaves the heart with each contraction.
Systemic circulation	The circulation of blood between the heart and the rest of the body.
Systole	The pressure in blood vessels as the heart is contracting.

Key Terms

Term	Definition
Thrombocytes	Platelets that allow blood to clot.
Venipuncture	The placement of a needle or catheter directly into a blood vessel to administer drugs or intravenous fluids and to withdraw blood.
Ventricles	The lower chambers of the heart, which are the larger and more muscular cardiac chambers. There is a right and a left ventricle.

What Do You Remember?

Answer key on page 199

1. **________________ deliver nutrients and oxygen to cells.**

a. Capillaries
b. Arteries
c. Venules
d. Veins

2. **________________ carry deoxygenated blood to the heart.**

a. Arteries
b. Capillaries
c. Venules
d. Veins

3. **________________ circulation is the circulation of blood between the heart and the rest of the body.**

a. Pulmonary
b. Blood
c. Systemic
d. Heart

4. **A dog has been running and has a heart rate of 120 beats per minute and a stroke volume of 2.5 ml/minute. What is the dog's cardiac output?**

a. 500 ml
b. 400 ml
c. 300 ml
d. 200 ml

Answer key on page 199

What Do You Remember?

5. **______________ deliver oxygen to body tissues and remove carbon dioxide from them via the bloodstream.**

a. Electrolytes
b. Erythrocytes
c. Leukocytes
d. Thrombocytes

6. **______________ allow blood to clot to prevent excessive bleeding.**

a. Electrolytes
b. Erythrocytes
c. Leukocytes
d. Thrombocytes

7. **Plasma contains ______________.**

a. water, erythrocytes, and waste products
b. water, electrolytes, and proteins
c. water, leukocytes, and proteins
d. water, thrombocytes, and waste products

8. **The ___________ vein may be used for venipuncture in most large and small mammals.**

a. femoral
b. saphenous
c. cephalic
d. jugular

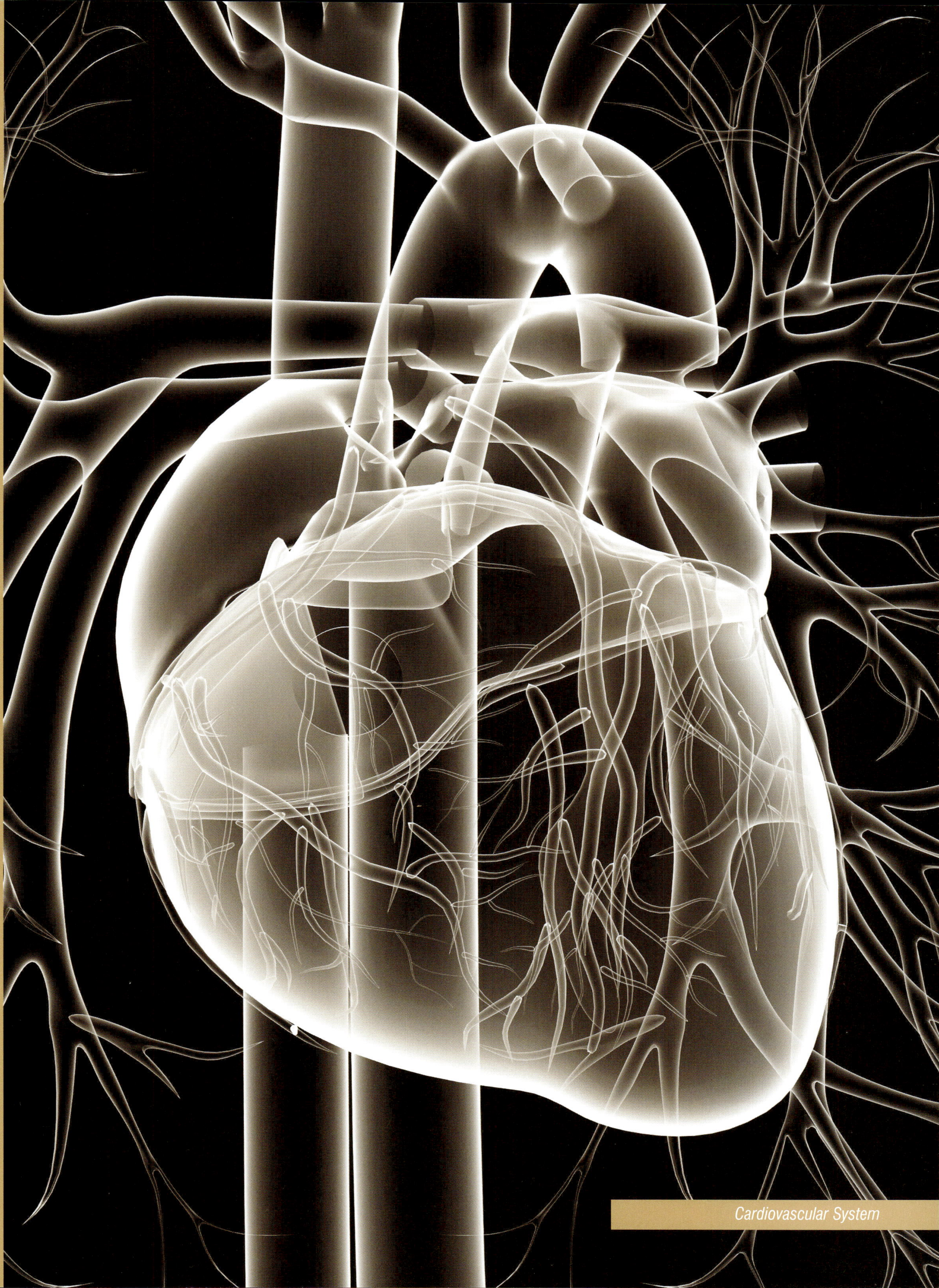

Cardiovascular System

Blood Vessel

CHAPTER 5

The Lymphatic System

Highlights of the Chapter

- The functions and organs of the lymphatic system
- The formation of lymph
- The lymphatic system and immunity

Introduction

The lymphatic system is a series of vessels that carry excess tissue fluid to blood vessels near the heart, where it is put back into the bloodstream. The lymphatic system also includes lymph tissue throughout the body in structures such as lymph nodes, the spleen, the thymus, the tonsils, and gut-associated lymph tissue (GALT).

The fluid carried by the lymphatic system is called lymph. Lymph is a clear, watery fluid that is similar to blood plasma, except that it contains large numbers of white blood cells called lymphocytes. It also contains nutrients and hormones.

The lymphatic system has four functions:

- *Removal of excess tissue fluid.* Lymph vessels drain fluid from specific areas of the body, much like veins return blood to the heart.
- *Waste material transport.* The fluid that enters the lymphatic capillaries will contain some of the waste materials from tissue cells that will be carried to the blood by lymph and eventually eliminated.

- *Filtration of lymph.* The fluid that enters the lymph capillaries also contains microorganisms, cellular debris, and other foreign matter that must be removed from lymph before it enters the bloodstream. As the lymph passes through the lymph nodes, these materials are filtered out.
- *Protein transport.* The lymph brings some large proteins, such as enzymes, to the bloodstream. These proteins are too large to enter the blood directly. Lymph is able to pick up larger protein molecules than capillaries and deposit them in the bloodstream.

The Organs of the Lymphatic System

Figure 5.1 Locations of Lymph Nodes in a Dog

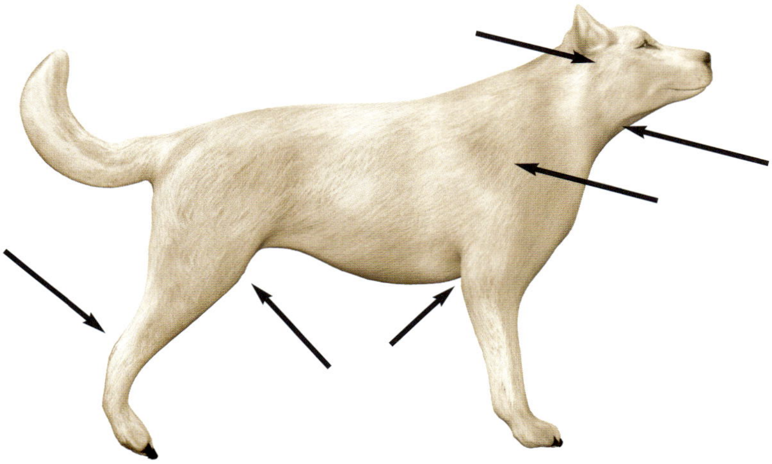

Lymph vessels are similar to veins. Both are thin-walled and return fluid to the right side of the heart. The movement of fluid in both is brought about by the contraction of the muscles that surround them and both have valves that prevent backflow. One important difference is that lymph passes through at least one lymph node before it reaches the blood system.

Lymph nodes are of various sizes and shapes and are found throughout the body, with clusters in the neck, the area where the foreleg attaches to the chest (equivalent to the human armpit), and the groin. They consist of lymph tissue surrounded by a fibrous sheath. Lymph flows into them through several incoming vessels. It then trickles through small channels where white blood cells called macrophages remove the bacteria and debris by engulfing and digesting them. The lymph then leaves the lymph nodes through outgoing vessels to continue its journey toward the heart, where it rejoins the blood circulation.

As well as filtering lymph, lymph nodes produce white blood cells called lymphocytes. The thymus gland, spleen, and bone marrow of long bones also produce lymphocytes. These cells attack pathogens and defend the body against them.

Lymph nodules are tiny lymph nodes that are usually found in the loose connective tissue beneath membranes lining various organ systems. Sites where lymph nodules are found include the digestive and respiratory systems, and the urinary bladder. Lymph nodules form in regions of frequent exposure to microorganisms or foreign materials and contribute to the defense against them. They frequently contain sites for the localized production of lymphocytes. Unlike lymph nodes, nodules do not have a well-defined connective-tissue capsule as a boundary and do not function as lymph filters.

The spleen is located on the left side of the abdomen caudal to the stomach. It is made of two different types of tissue. One tissue makes and stores lymphocytes. These lymphocytes can clone themselves during an immune response. The other tissue destroys worn out red blood cells, breaking down the hemoglobin into iron, which is recycled, and waste products that are excreted. The spleen also stores red blood cells. When severe blood loss occurs, it contracts and releases them into circulation.

The spleen is not essential for the life of an animal and can be surgically removed if necessary. Trauma resulting in the rupture of the spleen and tumors in the organ are the most common reasons for performing a splenectomy. After the surgery, tissue microphages and lymphoid tissue in other areas of the body will pick up most of the spleen's duties.

The thymus lies in the chest just under the sternum and cranial to the heart. The thymus processes lymphocytes, giving them the ability to recognize and attack foreign invaders, such as bacteria. In young animals, the thymus starts the normal development of the immune system.

Gut-associated lymph tissue (GALT) is a general term for the lymphoid tissue found in the lining of the digestive tract (stomach, intestines, esophagus) and the appendix. GALT stores lymphocytes and functions as the digestive tract's immune system.

The tonsils are masses of lymphatic tissue located inside the mouth and at the back of the throat. They help prevent the spread of infection in the respiratory system by protecting the body from bacteria and other harmful substances that enter the nose and throat. Tonsils are most prominent in young animals as they are developing their immune systems.

The Formation of Lymph

Lymph starts out as excess tissue fluid that is picked up directly from tissues by small lymph capillaries. This fluid is blood plasma that brings nutrients, oxygen, and hormones to cells and tissues. Excess tissue fluid accumulates when more fluid leaves blood capillaries than re-enters them. If it were not for lymph vessels, the body's tissues would all swell with excess fluid.

Tiny lymph capillaries join together to form large lymph vessels. Lymph vessels pass through lymph nodes, where they pick up lymphocytes. Any microorganisms in the lymph are removed from it by macrophages in the lymph nodes. The lymph vessels eventually join to form the lymphatic duct on the right side and the thoracic duct on the left. These large ducts empty lymph into veins in the upper thoracic cavity.

Figure 5.2 Lymph Node

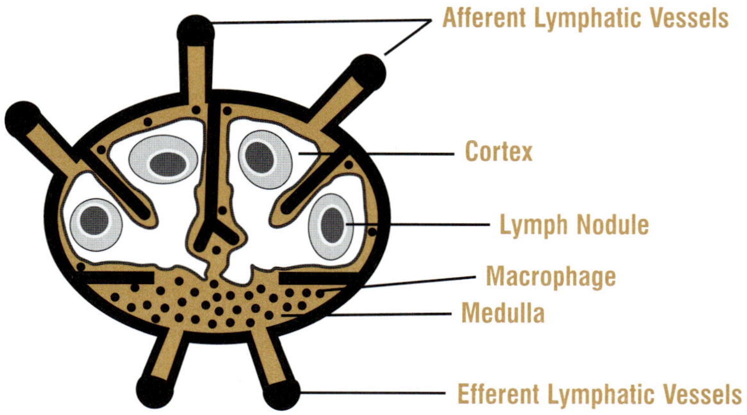

The Lymphatic System and Immunity

There are three types of lymphocytes: T lymphocytes (T cells), B lymphocytes (B cells), and natural killer cells. T lymphocytes are processed in the thymus before going on to the lymph nodes and other peripheral lymphoid tissue. T cells are responsible for cell-mediated immunity and activating B cells.

T cells develop specific receptors to antigens, or foreign proteins, on their cell membranes. These receptors are unique for one antigen only. T cells will either attach to antigenic cells and destroy them directly or secrete a chemical messenger, which acts as a poison to quickly kill any cell it attacks. The cells attacked by T cells are usually cells that have been invaded by viruses or are cancerous.

Inactive B cells travel through lymph nodes, the spleen, and other structures in the lymphatic system, but rarely circulate in the bloodstream. B cells are responsible for antibody production. Each B cell is preprogrammed to produce only one specific antibody against one specific antigen. When B cells recognize an antigen, they turn into plasma cells that release antibodies. An animal's body can produce over 100 trillion antibodies.

Both T cells and B cells can become memory cells. These cells are clones of an original lymphocyte. They don't participate in an initial immune response to an antigen. Instead, they live in lymphoid tissue waiting for a second exposure to the same antigen. When the animal is exposed to that antigen the second time, the memory cells respond to protect the body from it. The second immune response is quicker and stronger than the initial immune response.

Natural killer cells have the ability to kill some types of tumor cells and cells infected with various viruses. They don't have to be activated by a specific antigen, but they must come in direct contact with these cells before they can destroy them.

When an infection occurs in the body, the lymph nodes often become swollen and tender because of their increased activity. The lymph nodes at the site of the infection become larger due to the increased production of lymphocytes and macrophages, which will attempt to remove the microorganisms causing the infection. If enlarged, lymph nodes can provide a clue about where an infection is located.

The lymphatic system performs many actions to fight off disease and keep an animal healthy. But when things go wrong with the body's immune system, the lymphatic system may actually contribute to the spread of disease—particularly cancer. Sometimes, due to abnormalities in the genetic material of cells, cancerous cells display uncontrolled growth and start to invade adjacent tissues. Eventually, a tumor forms. Cancer cells can break away from the malignant tumor and be carried to the lymph nodes and then transported to other parts of the body, where they multiply to form a second growth. This is called "metastasis" and is how the lymphatic system can contribute to the spread of cancer. Cancer cells may also spread to lymph nodes near the primary tumor.

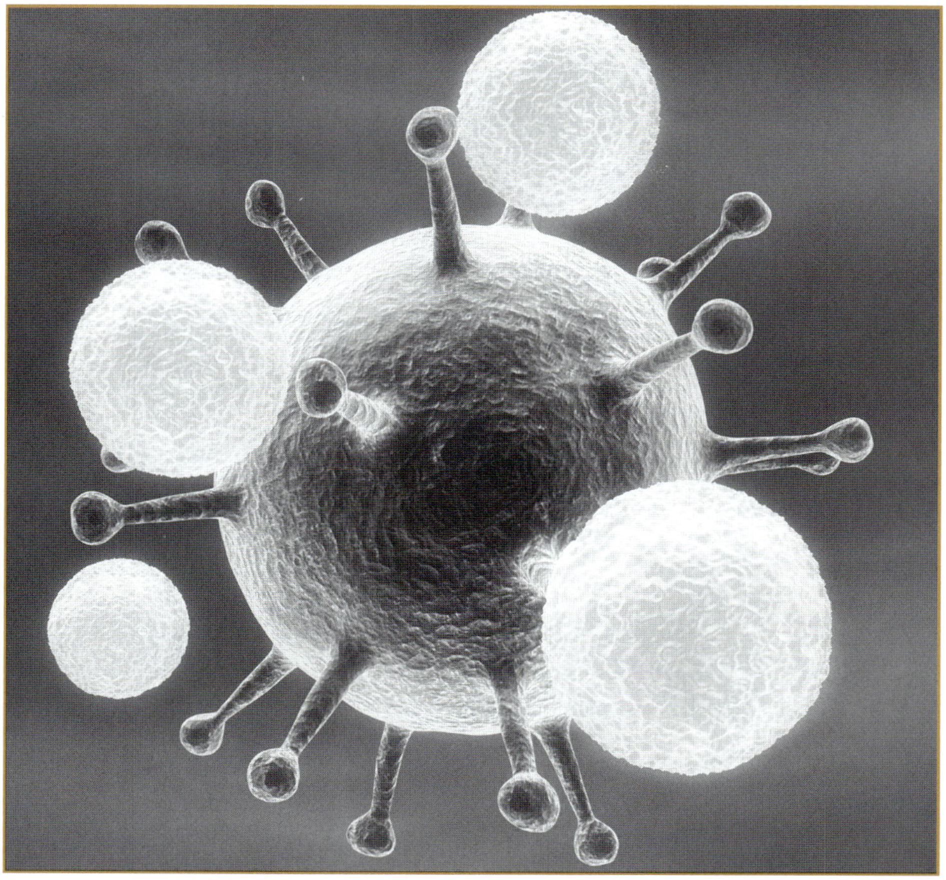

Summary

The lymphatic system has four functions:

- Removing excess tissue fluid
- Transporting waste materials from cells to the blood
- Filtering lymph to remove foreign matter
- Transporting protein to the blood

Lymph is a clear, watery fluid that contains a large number of lymphocytes. The organs of the lymphatic system include lymph vessels that carry lymph to the heart, and lymph nodes that filter out foreign matter from it. Lymph nodules are tiny lymph nodes that are usually found in the loose connective tissue beneath membranes lining various organ systems. They frequently contain sites for the localized production of lymphocytes.

The spleen and bone marrow of long bones make and store lymphocytes. The thymus processes lymphocytes, giving them the ability to recognize and attack foreign invaders. Gut-associated lymph tissue (GALT) is found in the lining of the digestive system and the appendix. GALT stores lymphocytes and functions as the digestive tract's immune system.

Key Terms

Term	Definition
Antigen	A substance that prompts the generation of antibodies and can cause an immune response. Examples are viruses, bacteria, and fungi.
B cell	A lymphocyte that makes antibodies against antigens.
Cell-mediated immunity	A branch of the immune system that uses defense cells (T lymphocytes, killer cells, macrophages, and other white blood cells) rather than antibodies to attack foreign invaders. Viruses will invade the cells of their animal hosts to hide from antibody-making cells. Cell-mediated immunity, rather than antibodies, must be used to kill these cells.
Gut-associated lymph tissue (GALT)	A general term for the lymphoid tissue found in the lining of the digestive tract and the appendix. GALT stores lymphocytes and functions as the digestive tract's immune system.
Lymph capillaries	Tiny thin-walled vessels that are closed at one end and that drain excess tissue fluid from tissues so that it can be filtered and returned to the bloodstream.
Lymph nodes	Organs found throughout the body that filter foreign particles from lymph and produce lymphocytes.
Lymph nodules	Tiny lymph nodes that are usually found in the loose connective tissue beneath membranes lining various organ systems.
Lymphatic duct	Lymph vessel that drains lymph from the right thoracic cavity, right limb, and right side of the head and neck. All other parts of the body are drained by the thoracic duct.

Key Terms

Term	Definition
Lymphocyte	A type of white blood cell in the immune system. Lymphocytes include natural killer cells, T cells, and B cells.
Macrophage	A type of white blood cell that engulfs and digests cellular debris and pathogens.
Metastasis	The process by which cancer spreads from the place at which it first arose as a primary tumor to other locations in the body.
Natural killer cell	A lymphocyte that defends the body from cancerous and virally infected cells.
Spleen	An organ of the lymphatic system located on the left side of the abdomen near the stomach which produces lymphocytes, stores red blood cells, and destroys old red blood cells.
Splenectomy	Surgical removal of the spleen.
T cell	A lymphocyte involved in cell-mediated immunity and activating B cells.
Thoracic duct	The largest lymph vessel in the body which collects most of the lymph and drains it into the bloodstream.
Thymus	An organ of the lymphatic system located in the chest behind the sternum. It processes lymphocytes, turning them into T cells with the ability to recognize and attack foreign invaders.
Tonsils	Two immune system glands located inside the mouth and at the back of the throat.

What Do You Remember?

Answer key on page 199

1. **Which of the following organs produce(s) lymphocytes?**

a. spleen
b. lymph nodes
c. thymus gland
d. both a and b

2. **The __________ processes lymphocytes so that they can attack foreign invaders.**

a. thymus gland
b. lymph nodes
c. lymph nodules
d. spleen

3. **__________ are the white blood cells that produce antibodies against antigens.**

a. T cells
b. B cells
c. Killer cells
d. Macrophages

4. **______________ engulf and digest cellular debris and pathogens.**

a. T cells
b. B cells
c. Killer cells
d. Macrophages

5. **Which of the following types of white blood cells can become memory cells?**

a. macrophages
b. B cells
c. T cells
d. both b and c

Answer key on page 199

What Do You Remember?

6. The MAIN difference between lymph and blood plasma is that lymph contains ____________.

a. lymphocytes
b. proteins
c. nutrients
d. hormones

7. Unlike lymph nodes, lymph nodules ________________________.

a. do not produce lymphocytes
b. do not filter lymph
c. are not located along a lymph vessel
d. both b and c

Jack Russell Terrier

CHAPTER 6

The Respiratory System

Highlights of the Chapter

- The functions and organs of the respiratory system
- How breathing occurs
- Pulmonary circulation
- Respiratory infections

Introduction

An animal's respiratory system includes its nose, sinuses, nasal chambers, epiglottis, larynx, trachea, and lungs. It provides oxygen to an animal's bloodstream so that oxygenated blood can reach its tissues. The body's cells need a constant energy supply to burn nutrients to produce energy. The respiratory system also transports carbon dioxide away from an animal's cells as a waste product. These vital processes are carried out by the respiratory system working together with the cardiovascular system.

There are two types of respiration:

- External respiration: air is exchanged between the external environment and the lungs
- Internal respiration: an exchange of oxygen and carbon dioxide between the cells and the blood

In addition to its primary function of swapping oxygen for carbon dioxide, or breathing, the respiratory system has some secondary functions. These include voice production and body temperature regulation, as well as playing a role in the sense of smell.

Voice production begins in the larynx, or voice box. Two connective tissue bands, called the vocal cords, stretch across the larynx and vibrate as air passes over them. This produces the basic sound of the animal's voice. Other structures contribute resonance and other characteristics to vocal sounds. These include the chest cavity, nose, mouth, throat, and sinuses.

Body temperature regulation involves many body systems, including the respiratory system. In cold weather, blood vessels in the nasal passages help to warm inhaled air before it reaches the lungs. This helps prevent hypothermia by not chilling the blood circulating through the lungs. In hot weather, the respiratory system helps keep an animal cool through the mechanism of panting.

The sense of smell, called the olfactory sense, is very important to many animals. The receptors for the sense of smell are in sensory tissue located up high in the nasal passages. More information on the sense of smell can be found in chapter 9, "The Nervous and Sensory Systems."

This chapter will provide an overview of the respiratory system. For more details on the system and its components, see *The Veterinary Assistant Career and Medical Terminology* (chapter 7, "Essential Life Support").

The Organs of the Respiratory System

The organs of the respiratory system are contained in the thoracic, or chest, cavity, which is also called the thorax. The thorax is bounded by the thoracic vertebrae, as well as the ribs and sternum. It houses the lungs, heart, large blood vessels, trachea, and esophagus. A thin membrane called the pleura covers the organs and structures in the thorax and lines the inside of this cavity. The mediastinum is the part of the thorax between the lungs. It contains the heart and most of the other thoracic organs.

All of the respiratory organs and structures other than the lungs are part of the upper respiratory tract. All of the structures within the lungs are part of the lower respiratory tract.

The Upper Respiratory Tract

The upper respiratory tract includes the nose, pharynx (throat), larynx (voice box), and trachea (wind pipe).

Table 6.1 The Parts of the Upper Respiratory Tract

Organ or Part	Definition
Epiglottis	A flap of connective tissue that closes over the larynx during swallowing.
Glottis	The opening into the larynx.
Larynx	Air passageway that connects the pharynx to the trachea. The larynx contains the vocal cords. It has three functions: voice production, prevention of foreign material being inhaled, and control of airflow to and from the lungs.
Nasal passages	The nasal passages are located between the nostrils and the pharynx.
Nose	Nostrils provide the entrance to the respiratory system. The nose also contains organs for the sense of smell.
Pharynx	A part of the neck and throat that is a passageway to both the respiratory and digestive systems. The pharynx opens into the esophagus (digestive passageway) and the larynx (respiratory passageway).
Sinuses	Air spaces between the bones of the skull which have a similar lining to nasal passages to sweep mucus produced in the sinuses down into nasal passages. Each sinus is named after the skull bone that houses it. Most animals have two frontal sinuses and two maxillary sinuses, within the frontal and maxillary (upper jaw) bones.
Trachea	A tube that extends from the neck to the chest. Also known as the "windpipe."

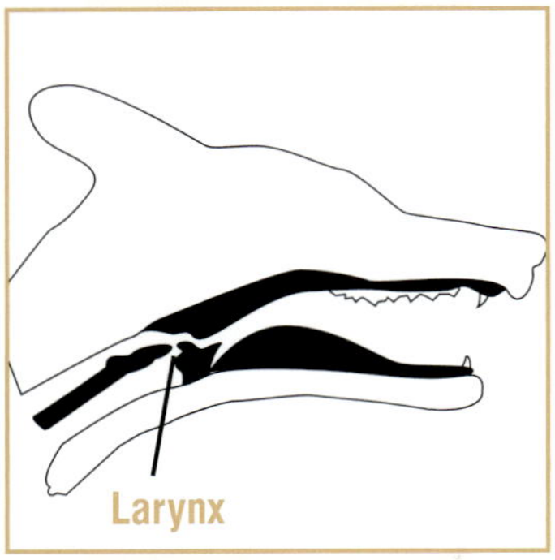

Swallowing and Breathing

Because the pharynx is a common passageway for both breathing and swallowing, reflexes must control the action of the muscles around the pharynx to prevent choking. The larynx and the pharynx must work together to prevent swallowing from interfering with breathing, and vice versa.

During breathing, the process is relatively simple: the larynx stays open to allow airflow. During swallowing, the process of breathing is stopped and the epiglottis closes over the larynx like a trap door. This keeps food out of the larynx and helps to direct it into the opening of the esophagus. The chewed food to be swallowed is moved to the rear of the pharynx and then into and down the esophagus. Once swallowing is complete, the opening of the larynx is uncovered and breathing resumes.

Most of the time, the reflexes involved in breathing and swallowing work well and we don't even notice them. Sometimes, however, these reflexes are not fast enough to prevent food or liquid from entering the larynx, resulting in choking.

The Lower Respiratory Tract

The lower respiratory tract starts with the bronchi that lead into the lungs and end with the alveoli where gas exchange occurs. Except for the two main bronchi that branch off from the trachea, all of the structures of the lower respiratory tract are found in the lungs.

The lungs fill most of the thoracic cavity. In most domestic animals, the left lung is divided into three lobes (cranial, middle, and caudal) and the right lung into four lobes (cranial, middle, caudal, and a small accessory lobe).

The air passageways that lead from the bronchi to the alveoli are often called the bronchial tree, because they divide into smaller and smaller passageways similar to the branching of a tree. After they enter the lungs, the bronchi branch into smaller bronchi and, finally, into tiny bronchioles. Bronchioles continue to subdivide into the smallest air passageways—the alveoli.

Table 6.2 The Parts of the Lower Respiratory Tract

Organ or Part	Definition
Alveoli	Tiny, thin-walled air sacs found at the end of bronchioles.
Bronchi	The two sections of the trachea that enter the lungs.
Bronchioles	Smaller branches of the bronchi.
Lungs	Organs whose principal function is to transport oxygen from the atmosphere into the bloodstream and release carbon dioxide from the bloodstream into the atmosphere.

How Breathing Occurs

Inspiration is when an animal breathes air into its lungs, or inhales; expiration is when an animal breathes out, or exhales.

The main muscles involved in inspiration are the external intercostal muscles and the diaphragm. The diaphragm is a dome-like sheet of muscle that separates the thoracic and abdominal cavities. The external intercostal muscles are located in the external portion of the spaces between the ribs.

Figure 6.1 The Breathing Process

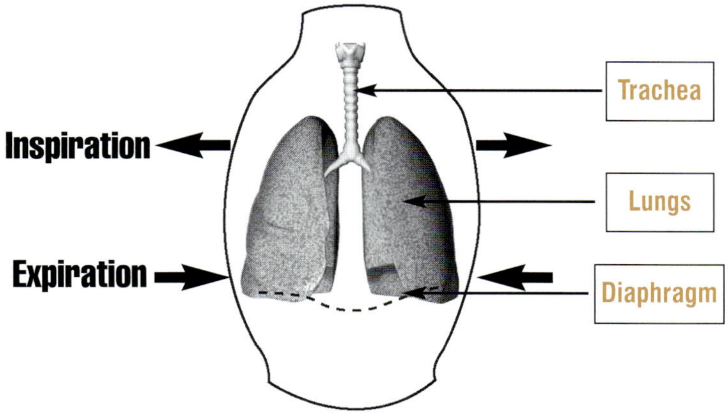

During inspiration, the diaphragm and intercostal muscles enlarge the volume of the chest. When it contracts, the diaphragm enlarges the chest cavity by flattening its dome shape. When the external intercostal muscles contract, they enlarge the chest by pushing the ribs upward and forward. The lifting of the ribs is also aided by some of the muscles of the shoulder, neck, and chest that attach to the rib cage. The lungs follow passively, and air is drawn into them through the respiratory passages.

During expiration, the size of the chest cavity is reduced. This compresses the lungs and pushes air out through the respiratory passages. The main muscles involved in expiration are the internal intercostal and abdominal muscles. The internal intercostal muscles are located between the ribs. When these muscles contract, they pull the ribs backward, which helps push the air out of the lungs. When abdominal muscles contract, they push the abdominal organs against the floor of the diaphragm. This pushes the diaphragm back into its full dome shape and decreases the size of the thorax.

The respiratory system functions as a bellows, pulling air into the lungs during inspiration and blowing it back out during expiration.

Respiration is controlled by a respiratory center in the brain stem located at the base of the brain. The respiratory center sends nerve impulses to the respiratory muscles telling them when and how much to contract. When the lungs are full, another nerve impulse is sent out to stop the muscle contractions that have been producing inspiration and start those that will produce expiration.

Figure 6.2 The Brain Controls Respiration

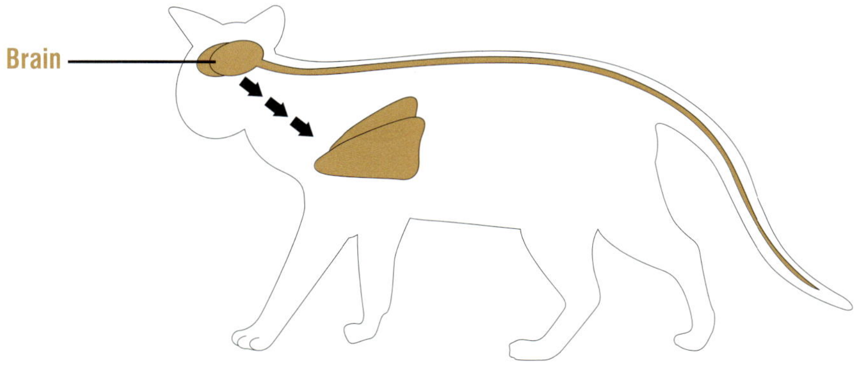

Pulmonary Circulation

The blood supply to and from the lungs is called pulmonary circulation. After delivering oxygen to the body's cells and picking up the carbon dioxide that was produced, carbon dioxide–rich blood enters the right side of the heart and is pumped into the pulmonary artery by the right ventricle. The pulmonary artery splits into the left and right pulmonary arteries that enter the two lungs. Within the lungs, the blood vessels follow and subdivide along with the bronchi. When blood enters the capillary networks around the alveoli, it gets rid of its carbon dioxide and picks up oxygen. Next, the oxygen-rich blood enters the pulmonary venules, which join together into increasingly larger blood vessels to form the pulmonary veins that leave each lung and enter the heart's left side. The blood is then pumped back into systemic circulation to supply the body with oxygen.

Respiratory Infections

Respiratory tract infections are common in all animals. From a medical standpoint, respiratory infections are separated into those that affect the upper respiratory tract and those that affect the lower respiratory tract. An upper respiratory tract infection may affect some combination of the nasal passages, pharynx, larynx, and trachea. A lower respiratory tract infection affects the lungs.

Upper respiratory track infections are less likely to be serious and life threatening than those of the lower respiratory track. Why? The main reason is that the body is able to drain excess mucus and fluids away from affected areas. The fluids can be coughed up and expelled through the nose or mouth. For this reason, a moist cough is referred to as a productive cough because it helps the animal to get better.

A lower respiratory tract infection is usually called either bronchitis or pneumonia. Bronchitis affects the lining of the bronchial tree. It occurs when the trachea (windpipe) and the airways within the lungs become inflamed because of infection, causing coughing, wheezing, and difficulty with breathing.

Pneumonia affects the bronchioles and alveoli, causing inflammation and the abnormal filling of fluid. Pneumonia can be caused by infection by bacteria, viruses, fungi, or parasites, or chemical or physical injury to the lungs. It leads to coughing, chest pain, fever, and shortness of breath.

With both bronchitis and pneumonia, inflammatory fluids tend to accumulate deep in the lungs in air passageways. This makes the fluids more difficult to cough up, so they often accumulate and obstruct airflow. These complications make pneumonia and bronchitis more serious and debilitating illnesses than upper respiratory tract infections. Pneumonia can cause death in an elderly or chronically ill animal. Animals showing symptoms of either pneumonia or bronchitis should receive prompt veterinary care.

Summary

The respiratory system's main functions are to provide the body's cells with a constant supply of oxygen and to transport carbon dioxide away from cells as a waste product. Its secondary functions include voice production and assisting with body temperature regulation and the sense of smell.

The respiratory system is divided into the upper respiratory tract containing the nose, pharynx, larynx, and trachea, and the lower respiratory tract containing the lungs and associated structures.

The two bronchi branch off from the trachea and lead into the right and left lungs. Air passageways branching off from the bronchi within the lungs become increasing smaller. The bronchioles are smaller branches of the bronchi. Bronchioles lead to the alveoli, the tiny air sacs surrounded by networks of capillaries where gas exchange with the blood occurs.

Respiration is an automatic process controlled by the respiratory center in the base of the brain. The respiratory center sends nerve impulses to the respiratory muscles, telling them when and how much to contract.

Inspiration occurs when an animal breathes air into its lungs, or inhales; expiration occurs when an animal breathes out, or exhales. During inspiration, the diaphragm and external intercostal muscles in the chest contract to enlarge the chest cavity. During expiration, the internal intercostal muscles in the chest and abdominal muscles contract, reducing the size of the chest cavity and helping to push air out of the lungs.

Key Terms

Term	Definition
Bronchitis	Inflammation of the trachea and bronchi, causing deep and painful coughing that brings up phlegm.
Diaphragm	The principle muscle involved in breathing; separates the thoracic and abdominal cavities.
Expiration	Exhaling air from the lungs.
External intercostal muscles	The chest muscle involved in inspiration (inhaling); located in the external portion of the spaces between the ribs.
External respiration	The process of exchanging air between the external environment and the lungs.
Inspiration	Inhaling air into the lungs.
Internal intercostal muscles	The chest muscle involved in expiration (exhaling); located between the ribs.
Internal respiration	The process of exchanging oxygen and carbon dioxide at the cellular level, between the cells and the blood.
Mediastinum	The part of the thoracic cavity between the lungs, which contains the heart, trachea, and esophagus.
Olfactory sense	The sense of smell.
Pleura	A thin membrane covering the organs of the thoracic cavity and lining the cavity itself.
Pneumonia	Inflammation of the bronchioles and alveoli and abnormal filling of liquid of the alveoli.
Pulmonary circulation	The circulation of blood between the heart and the lungs.

Key Terms

Term	Definition
Respiratory system	The body system that includes the lungs and provides oxygen to an animal's bloodstream.
Systemic circulation	The circulation of blood between the heart and the rest of the body.
Thoracic cavity	The chest cavity bounded by the thoracic vertebrae, ribs, and sternum, which contains the heart and the respiratory organs. Also called the thorax.

Answer key on page 199

What Do You Remember?

1. **Within the lungs, the exchange of oxygen and carbon dioxide occurs in the ______________.**

a. bronchioles
b. bronchial tree
c. alveoli
d. bronchi

2. **The main muscles involved in inspiration are the ______________ and the ______________.**

a. diaphragm, external intercostal muscles
b. diaphragm, internal intercostal muscles
c. abdominal muscles, external intercostal muscles
d. abdominal muscles, internal intercostal muscles

3. **Which of the following organs and body structures is NOT housed in the thoracic cavity?**

a. heart
b. lungs
c. trachea
d. diaphragm

4. **______________ is another word for pharynx.**

a. Voice box
b. Wind pipe
c. Throat
d. Nasal passage

What Do You Remember?

Answer key on page 199

5. **During swallowing, the __________closes over the __________ to prevent choking.**

a. glottis, pharynx
b. glottis, larynx
c. epiglottis, trachea
d. epiglottis, larynx

6. **Which of the following sequences correctly shows how air enters the lungs?**

a. trachea → bronchioles → bronchi → alveoli
b. trachea → bronchi → bronchioles → alveoli
c. trachea → bronchi → alveoli → bronchioles
d. trachea → alveoli → bronchi → bronchioles

7. **Lower respiratory tract infections tend to be more serious and life-threatening than upper respiratory tract infections because they __________.**

a. cause respiratory failure
b. inflame sensitive lung tissue
c. cause fluid to accumulate in air passageways, obstructing airflow
d. are always caused by harmful bacteria

8. **Pneumonia primarily affects the __________ lobes of the lungs.**

a. cranial
b. caudal
c. middle
d. both b and c

Constantine, Norwegian Fjord

CHAPTER 7

The Digestive System

Highlights of the Chapter

- The organs of the digestive system and their function
- The digestive process
- How nutrients are absorbed
- How the digestive systems of herbivores, carnivores, and omnivores differ
- The monogastric (single-chambered) and ruminant (four-chambered) stomachs
- Nutrients and metabolism

Introduction

The digestive system has two main jobs. First, it breaks down food to make energy for the body. Second, it eliminates solid waste products from the body.

The digestive tract runs from the mouth, or oral cavity, to the anus. It includes the digestive organs that carry out the processes of digestion and absorption of nutrients. It is also called the gastrointestinal tract, the alimentary canal, or simply the gut.

Domestic animals have different types of digestive systems, depending on whether or not they are carnivores, herbivores, or omnivores. This chapter will provide an overview of how different animals process the nutrients they need to stay healthy.

The Parts of the Digestive System

The digestive system lies within an animal's abdominal and pelvic cavities. An animal's digestive tract includes its esophagus, gall bladder, liver, stomach, pancreas, small and large intestines, and oral cavity. These organs will briefly be presented here. A complete description of the functions of different parts of the digestive system can be found in Table 8.1 of *The Veterinary Assistant Career and Medical Terminology* (page 140).

Figure 7.1 Digestive System

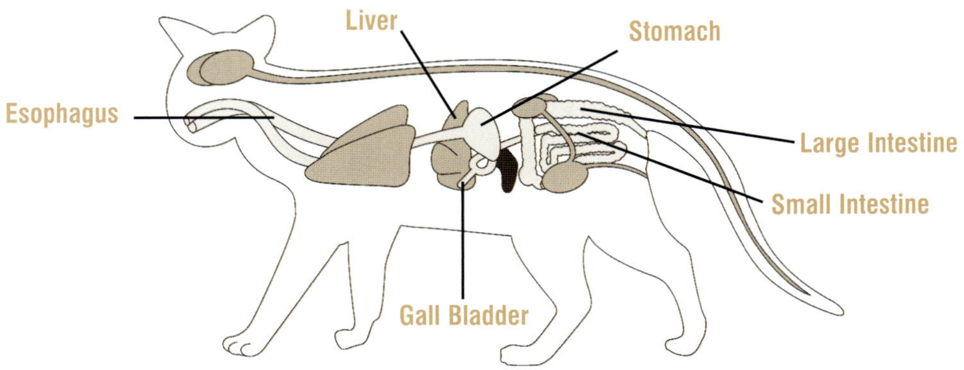

The Oral Cavity

The oral cavity is where food is taken in and digestion begins. Its purpose is to take hold of food (with the lips), chew it (with teeth), and prepare the food for swallowing (with saliva). The tongue manipulates food during chewing and swallowing.

Salivary glands aid in digestion by producing saliva, which moistens, lubricates, and softens food. Saliva also lubricates and protects the teeth, the tongue, and the tender tissues inside the mouth.

Teeth are responsible for physically breaking down food into smaller pieces through chewing, or mastication. This increases the surface area of food that is exposed to digestive processes. Mastication is also called mechanical digestion.

The teeth of carnivorous animals are shaped differently than the teeth of herbivores. Carnivore teeth are typically more pointed on the surfaces where the upper and lower teeth come together and slightly curved toward the back of the mouth. This makes it easier for carnivores to hold their prey and to tear, cut, and shred meat. Herbivores have teeth with mostly flat surfaces where the teeth come together, which helps them to grind plant material and grains. Herbivore teeth are also straight, rather than curved.

Both carnivore and herbivore teeth are classified as follows:

- Incisors (grasping teeth), at the front of the mouth
- Canines (tearing teeth), at the corners of the incisors
- Premolars (cutting teeth), at the side of the mouth next to the canine teeth
- Molars (grinding teeth), the most caudal teeth, located at the cheek

Canines are typically longer than the other teeth and are pointed at the tip. The premolars have some sharp points and surfaces in carnivorous species. The molars have larger, flatter surfaces and are used by all species for grinding.

Cattle and other ruminant species have six incisors and two canine teeth in their lower jaw, but no upper incisors or canine teeth. Instead, they have a dental pad, which is a thick, connective-tissue structure on the upper jaw opposite the lower incisors and canine teeth.

Figure 7.2 The Lower Jaw Teeth

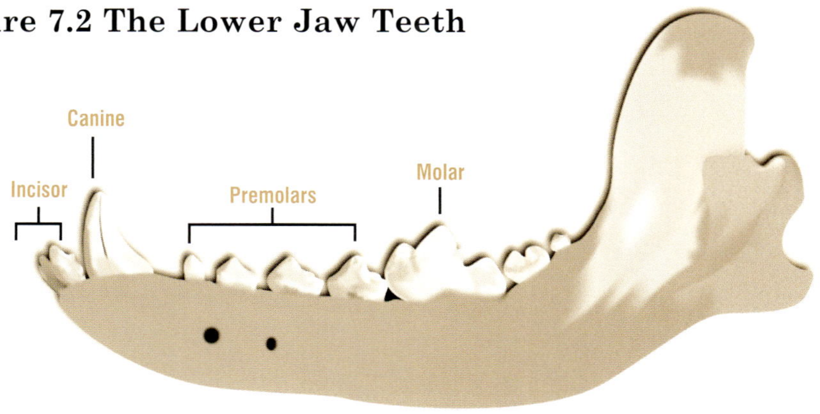

Table 7.1 Dental Formulas for Domestic Species

Species	Dental Formula	Total Number of Teeth
Puppy	12 incisors 4 canines 12 premolars	28
Adult dog	12 incisors 4 canines 16 premolars 10 molars	42
Kitten	12 incisors 4 canines 10 premolars	26
Adult cat	12 incisors 4 canines 10 premolars 4 molars	30
Adult horse	12 incisors 4 canines 12–14 premolars 12 molars	40–42
Adult pig	12 incisors 4 canines 16 premolars 12 molars	44
Adult cow	6 incisors 2 canines 12 premolars 12 molars	32

The Digestive Process

The mechanical digestion of food begins in the mouth. During swallowing, the pharynx moves food downward into the esophagus. Finally, through a series of involuntary contractions, food is pushed down into the stomach.

In the stomach, the mechanical process of digestion continues and chemical digestion begins, as acids and enzymes begin to break down the food. The food is changed into chyme, which is a semi-fluid mixture of partially digested food and secretions.

From the stomach, chyme moves into the small intestine, which has three parts:

- The duodenum
- The jejunum
- The ileum

Figure 7.3 Small Intestine

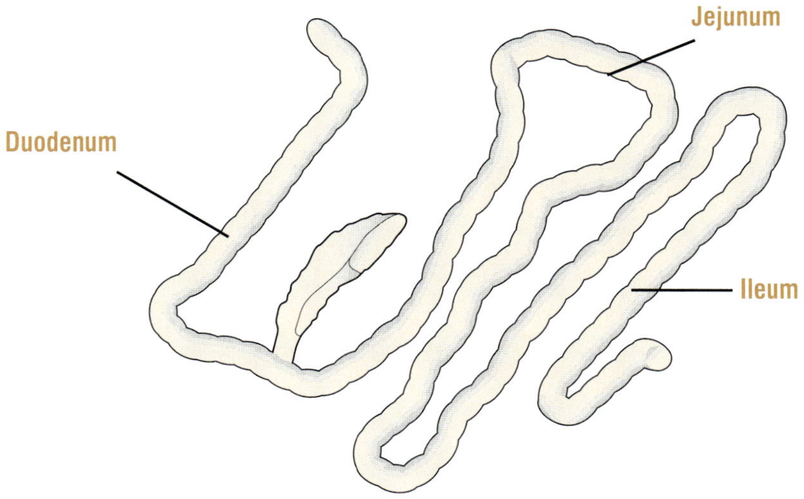

The liver, gallbladder, and pancreas produce chemicals that help the small intestine to digest food. Secretions from the pancreas and gall bladder enter the duodenum through the pancreatic and bile ducts.

The liver produces bile, which helps the body to digest fat and is stored in the gall bladder. The liver also filters materials absorbed from the digestive tract before they can reach systemic blood circulation. It contains phagocytes, or eating cells, which remove bacteria, toxins, poisons, old red blood cells, and infectious agents that enter the body through the walls of the digestive tract. In addition, such nutrients as glucose, amino acids, and some vitamins and minerals are either stored or metabolized by the liver.

The pancreas secretes the digestive enzymes amylase (which digests carbohydrates), proteases (which digest protein), and lipase (which digests fat) into the small intestine. It also secretes bicarbonate, which helps to neutralize the acidic contents coming from the stomach and maintain a pH in the duodenum at which pancreatic enzymes can function.

Most nutrients are absorbed into the bloodstream in the small intestine, through capillaries in its walls. Contractions within this organ churn chyme, ensuring that it is well mixed with digestive enzymes. Churning also brings digestive materials into contact with the intestinal tract's surface for absorption into the bloodstream. Food particles that cannot be absorbed through the small intestine move into the large intestine. The functions of the large intestine are to recover fluid and electrolytes and to store feces until they can be eliminated.

The large intestine has four parts:

- The cecum
- The colon
- The rectum
- The anus

The process of digestion and the absorption of nutrients is completed in the cecum, where the remaining waste products begin to be compacted. Compaction continues in the colon, which uses contractions to move body waste through it. The colon has many mucus-secreting glands that lubricate and aid the passage of its contents. The rectum acts as a temporary storage area for feces until they are excreted through the anus. The anus contains muscular sphincters that control the passage of fecal material.

Figure 7.4 Large Intestine

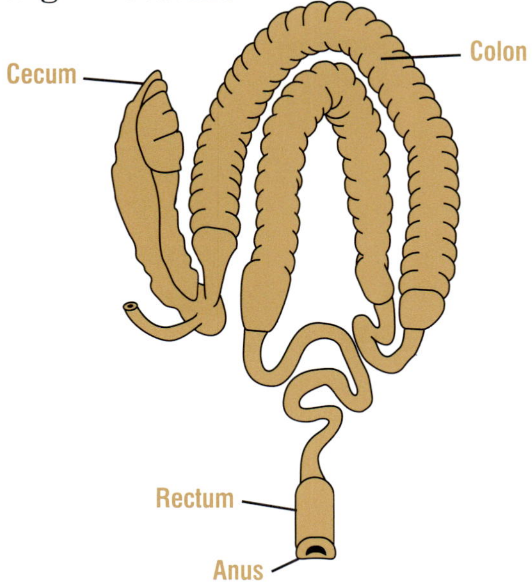

The process of excreting feces is called defecation. Many animals voluntarily decide when to defecate for purposes of living with humans and marking territory.

How Nutrients Are Absorbed

Carbohydrates, proteins, and fats are chemically digested in the small intestine with different enzymes. Amylase converts starch into smaller sugar segments called disaccharides, which means two sugars. Disaccharides include sucrose, maltose, and lactose. Other enzymes convert disaccharides into glucose, which is absorbed to supply the body with energy.

Proteins are large molecules that must be reduced to amino acids by protein-splitting enzymes called proteases. Because proteins have many different amino acids with different types of chemical bonds, many different proteases are required for the chemical digestion of protein.

Fats tend to clump together to form globules in the digestive system. To be properly digested, they must be chemically broken down through a process called emulsification. Agitation in the stomach breaks fat globules into small droplets. The emulsified fat droplets pass into the small intestine, where bile acids make the fat droplets water soluble.

Pancreatic lipases digest the fat molecules to produce fatty acids, glycerol, and monoglycerides (molecules containing glycerol and a single fatty acid), which are further broken down into small fragments that can be absorbed by the body.

An animal's ability to digest the nutrients provided by a particular diet will change with the diet itself. For example, if an animal that is used to being fed dry food is suddenly switched to moist food, its digestive system will not be able to process the sucrose normally added to moist pet food to improve taste and texture. This is because the animal's digestive system cannot produce enough of the enzyme that breaks down sucrose to chemically digest it. Initially, a large amount of the food will remain undigested, and the pet will have diarrhea. Within a few days, however, the pet's digestive system will produce enough enzymes to match the increased sugar content of the food.

Suddenly switching from dry to moist food or from one brand of pet food to another that may contain a different protein or carbohydrate will cause digestive problems. When switching diets, pet owners should gradually introduce the new food over a 5- to 7-day period. Doing so will allow the pet's digestive system to adjust gradually and avoid the problem of diarrhea.

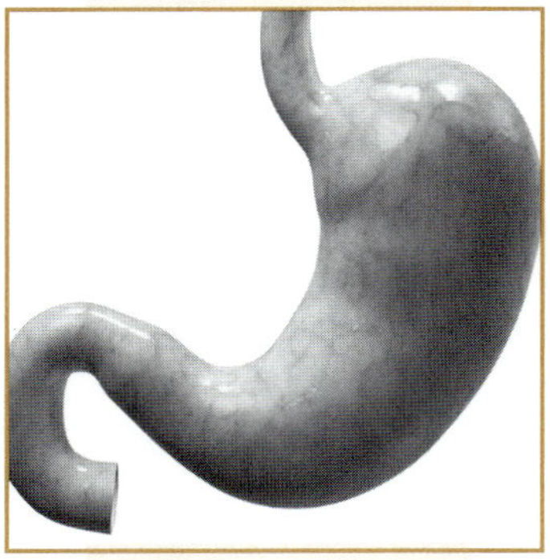

The Monogastric Stomach

The monogastric stomach is shaped like a C lying on its side. It is divided into five different areas: cardia, fundus, body, pyloric antrum, and pylorus. The cardia is the area immediately surrounding the opening from the esophagus into the stomach. The cardiac sphincter helps reduce reflux of stomach contents back into the esophagus. As the stomach fills with food, it acts as a valve to close the lower end of the esophagus. In some species, such as horses and rabbits, closure of the sphincter is so strong that reflux of stomach contents or vomiting is nearly impossible.

The fundus is the first of three areas where digestion takes place. It expands as more food is swallowed. The body forms the middle of the stomach. It also expands as food is eaten. The body contracts to help mix food. Both the fundus and the body have many gastric glands that produce digestive hydrochloric acid, digestive enzymes, and mucus, which forms a protective coating for the stomach. The mucous coating is essential for protecting stomach tissues from the harsh, highly acidic environment of the stomach. The mucus is alkaline, which helps to neutralize stomach acid.

The pyloric antrum is the distal part of the stomach. It grinds up swallowed food and regulates the acid produced by the stomach. It also produces mucus. The contractions of the pyloric antrum move food toward the pylorus.

The pylorus is a tubular, muscular organ that regulates the movement of chyme from the stomach into the duodenum. It also acts as a sphincter to prevent the backflow of chyme into the stomach from the small intestine. It remains partly open so that liquid can move into the duodenum, but solid and semisolid food is retained in the stomach.

The Ruminant Stomach

Figure 7.4 Ruminant Stomach

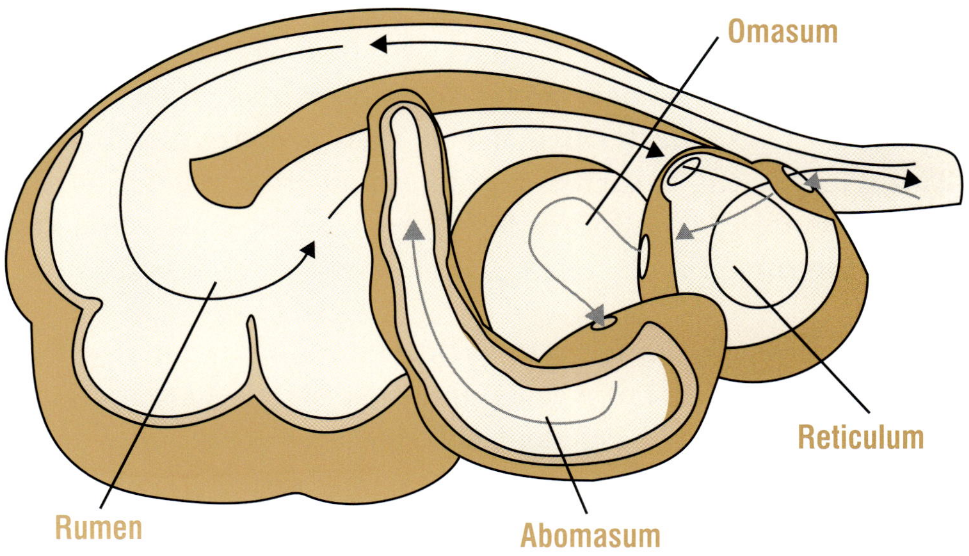

Cattle, sheep, and goats are ruminants. As the name implies, ruminants *ruminate* their food. This means that they regurgitate swallowed food, rechew it, and then swallow it again. This process is commonly referred to as "chewing the cud."

Each food bolus is chewed for about a minute and then swallowed again. Ruminants may spend 8 hours a day or more in rumination. This is achieved with a unique digestive system.

To help them digest large amounts of plant matter, ruminants have a stomach with four chambers. They have one true stomach called the abomasum, which is similar to the stomachs of monogastric animals, and three fore-stomachs—the reticulum, the rumen, and the omasum.

In the first two chambers, the rumen and the reticulum, the food is mixed with saliva and separated into solid and liquid material. Solids clump together to form the cud. The cud is then regurgitated and chewed slowly to completely mix it with saliva and to break down the particle size.

The reticulum and rumen also act as large fermentation vats, where bacteria and protozoa ferment rechewed plant material. The fermentation process produces methane gas, which must be expelled from the rumen to avoid excessive buildup of gas, or bloat.

The rumen is the largest compartment, storing large quantities of feed and mixing it with digestive bacteria through strong contractions. The rumen breaks down fiber in solid food particles into fatty acids, which cattle use as their primary metabolic fuel. This allows cattle to thrive on grasses and other vegetation. Fatty acids are absorbed into the body through finger-like projections lining the rumen wall.

The liver converts some fatty acids into glucose for use by the body's cells. Other fatty acids absorbed by the bloodstream are used to produce fat tissue and milk fat. The digestion of proteins also begins in the rumen.

Food then passes into the next chamber, the omasum, where water and any fatty acids not already digested are absorbed. Water and electrolytes are also absorbed in the omasum, drying out digested food before it enters the abomasum.

The abomasum is very similar to the human stomach. The wall of the abomasum secretes digestive enzymes and hydrochloric acid. The abomasum's main digestive function is the partial breakdown of proteins to peptides, which are short chains of amino acid molecules.

A ruminant's small intestine reduces any remaining proteins to amino acids, starch to glucose, and complex fats to fatty acids. These nutrients are then absorbed into the bloodstream in the lower half of the small intestine.

Nutrients and Metabolism

Most food consumed by animals is used for metabolic fuel. The nutrients obtained from eating are broken down into smaller molecules to be used for energy, growth, and cell repair. The amount of energy that can be acquired from these nutrient molecules is measured in calories.

A nutrient is a substance derived from food that the body uses to carry out its functions.

Nutrients are divided into six categories:

- Water
- Carbohydrates
- Fats
- Proteins
- Vitamins
- Minerals

Water, carbohydrates, fats, and proteins are consumed in large quantities. Vitamins and minerals are consumed in very small quantities. Carbohydrates, fats, and proteins produce energy, whereas water, vitamins, and minerals do not.

Table 7.2 Nutrient Groups and their Dietary Sources

Nutrient	Source
Carbohydrates	
■ Simple (sugars)	Fruit, honey, sugar cane, sugar beets, immature vegetables
■ Complex (starches)	Grains, nuts, rice, root vegetables, legumes
■ Complex (cellulose)	Most vegetables
Proteins	Meat, dairy products, legumes (beans, peas, lentils, soybeans), eggs
Fat	
■ Neutral fats	
• Saturated	Meat, dairy products
• Unsaturated	Seeds, nuts; vegetable, olive, and safflower oils
■ Cholesterol	Egg yolks, dairy products, animal fat
Other lipid substances	Dark leafy vegetables Root vegetables Some animal sources Fat-soluble vitamins

Water

Water is the most important nutrient in an animal's diet. Most animals cannot survive longer than a few days without it. Animals obtain water by ingesting food and drink and by oxidizing proteins, fats, and carbohydrates.

Water is used in almost all metabolic body processes. It is the major component of blood and lymph and is found inside and outside of cells. Water is a lubricant for body tissues. It is excreted as sweat and evaporated during panting to help regulate body temperature.

Carbohydrates

Carbohydrates are divided into three categories:

- Sugars, or simple carbohydrates
- Starches, or complex carbohydrates
- Cellulose, which is the complex carbohydrate found in the cell walls of vegetables. Ruminants are able to digest cellulose, but other animal species are not. In non-ruminant animals, cellulose becomes the dietary fiber, or roughage, that acts as the bulking agent for feces.

Glucose is the simplest and smallest form of dietary carbohydrate. Cells use it to make other molecules.

Neurons rely almost exclusively on glucose for their energy needs. That is why the brain is very sensitive to decreases in blood glucose levels. Even temporary decreases can depress brain function. Insulin released by the pancreas helps to provide the brain and other tissues with a steady level of glucose.

Fats and Lipids

Lipids are fat-soluble molecules used for a variety of vital body processes. Fats are a subgroup of lipids called triglycerides, which are formed when three fatty acids join with glycerol to form a molecule.

Lipids and fats may be divided into three categories:

- Neutral fats (saturated and non-saturated)
- Cholesterol
- Other lipid sources

Neutral fats are commonly referred to as "fats" when they are solid and "oils" when they are liquid. The two main types of neutral fats are saturated and unsaturated. Saturated fat is found in meat and dairy foods. Saturated fats are derived from animal sources and remain solid at room temperature. Unsaturated fat sources include seeds, nuts, and oils derived from vegetables and nuts. Unsaturated fats are derived from plants and some animal sources, such as fish. They are liquid at room temperature.

Saturated fat is known to raise blood cholesterol levels and is associated with heart disease. A healthy diet includes eating foods that contain more unsaturated fats than saturated fats—in other words, limiting intake of animal fat.

Neutral fats contain over twice the energy potential of proteins and carbohydrates. They are also easy to digest, make food taste good, stave off hunger for long periods, and enable the body to absorb the fat-soluble vitamins (A, D, E, and K). Stored fat in the body (adipose tissue) insulates animals from cold temperatures and cushions such organs as the heart, the kidneys, and the eyes.

Sources of cholesterol include egg yolks, meat, and dairy products. The liver is also able to manufacture this essential nutrient. Without it, animals would not be able to carry out many vital biochemical processes.

Other lipid substances are found in dark leafy vegetables, root vegetables, some animal sources, and fat-soluble vitamins. These substances are vital for an animal's survival. They include lipoproteins, which contain both proteins and lipids and enable the bloodstream to transport fat and cholesterol around the body. Cells use fats and cholesterol to build cellular membranes.

Proteins

The body uses proteins to make keratin, collagen, and elastin for the skin, hair, and nails; connective tissues; and muscles. Other proteins play roles in cell functions. For example, enzymes and hormones are proteins that regulate body functions. Hemoglobin is a protein that carries oxygen in red blood cells. Contractile proteins in muscle cells enable the body to move.

All proteins are made of amino acids. There are 22 different types of amino acids. Ten are essential, and 12 are nonessential. Essential amino acids must be included in an animal's diet because the animal either cannot make them at all or cannot make them fast enough to meet the body's needs for tissue maintenance and growth.

Animal products, such as meat, eggs, and dairy products, contain proteins that include the largest number of essential amino acids. Meat products contain all of the essential amino acids for many species. They are therefore called "complete proteins."

Cereals, rice, nuts, and legumes are rich in protein. But they are low in one or more of the essential amino acids, making them nutritionally incomplete. When eaten together, legumes, grains, and cereals provide all of the essential amino acids for many species, including humans. Together, these foods form a complete protein.

Pet foods often identify the crude protein content on the label. Many people assume that the best food for their pet contains the highest percentage of crude protein. However, this is not necessarily true. A pet food may have a high protein content, but the absorbable protein it provides for body functions may be low. The ideal protein content in pet food provides all of the essential amino acids a pet requires. This is often achieved by mixing animal and plant protein sources in food formulations.

Vitamins and Minerals

Unlike carbohydrates, proteins, and fats, vitamins do not produce energy when metabolized by the body. They are also not broken down into building block units.

Vitamins activate enzymes in the body and enable them to carry out their metabolic reactions. For example, the vitamins riboflavin and niacin are required to break down glucose chemically.

Other vitamins assist with body system and organ functioning. For example, vitamin D regulates calcium levels in the body and is essential for bone and tooth formation and blood clotting. Vitamin

A (retinal) helps the retina to detect light. Vitamin K is essential for the generation of blood clotting factors and many proteins made by the liver. Vitamin E is an important antioxidant and helps prevent damage to cell membranes.

Since most vitamins are not made in the body, they must be consumed in the diet. However, there are exceptions. Vitamin D is made by the skin when it is exposed to sunlight. Vitamin K and biotin are made in the intestine by bacteria. The body can also convert beta carotene, which is found in carrots and dark green leafy vegetables, into vitamin A.

Vitamins are either water- or fat-soluble, depending on how they are absorbed by the body. Water-soluble vitamins are absorbed through the intestinal wall into the bloodstream when water is absorbed from the digestive tract. Water-soluble vitamins include vitamin C and B-complex vitamins. Fat-soluble vitamins bind to ingested lipids, which are then absorbed through the intestinal tract. In order for an animal to digest fat-soluble vitamins and obtain their nutritional benefits, its diet must include some fat.

Minerals are inorganic substances that are essential to life. Like vitamins, minerals do not generate energy. Their role is to work with other nutrients to ensure that the body functions normally. For example, iodine is essential for normal thyroid function, which controls metabolic rate. Calcium, phosphorous, and magnesium harden teeth and bones. Sodium and chlorine help with water absorption in the kidneys. Iron is the core of the hemoglobin molecule that carries oxygen in red blood cells.

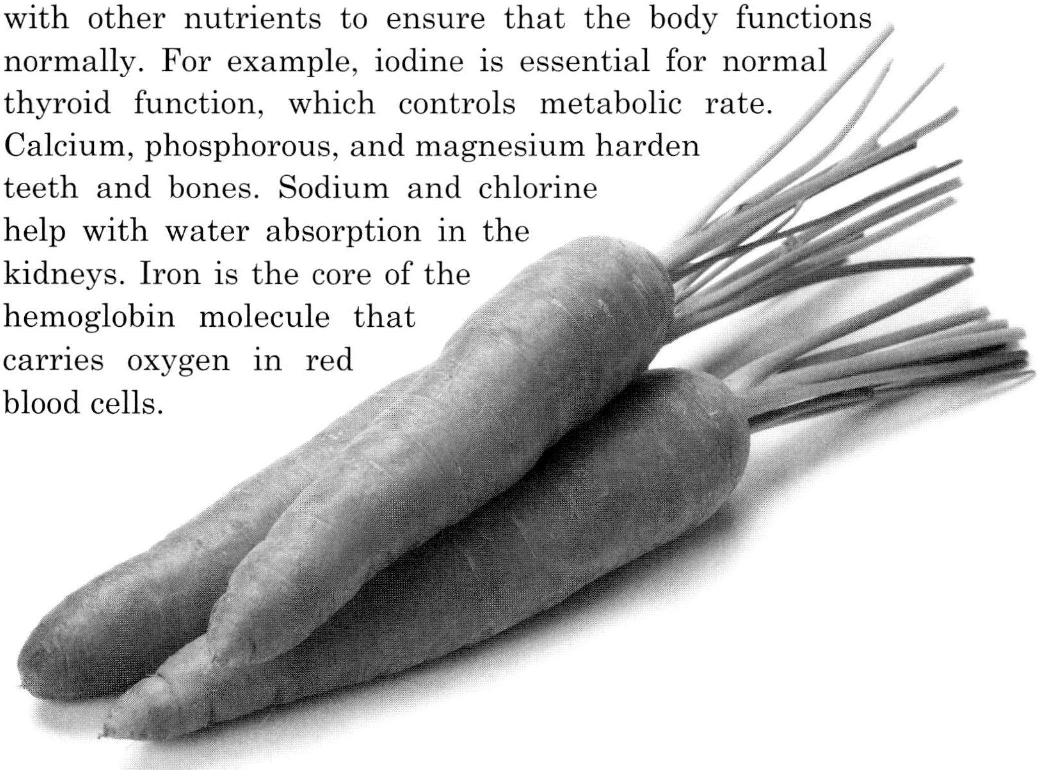

Summary

Digestion is the process of breaking down food into simpler chemical compounds that are capable of being absorbed by the small intestine. Carbohydrates are broken down into sugars, proteins into amino acids, and fats into fatty acids. These nutrients are used by the body for energy, growth, and cell repair.

Vitamins and minerals are other nutrients consumed in very small quantities that are essential to an animal's health. Unlike carbohydrates, proteins, and fats, vitamins and minerals do not produce energy when metabolized by the body. They are also not broken down into building block units.

Some vitamins activate enzymes in the body, enabling them to carry out their metabolic reactions. Others assist with body system and organ functioning. Minerals work with other nutrients to ensure that the body functions normally.

Digestion begins in the oral cavity, where food is chewed, covered with saliva, and swallowed. This is called mechanical digestion. Chewed food moves down the esophagus into the stomach, where the mechanical process of digestion continues through churning. Acids and enzymes turn the stomach into a semi-fluid mixture of partially digested food.

The chemical digestion of food continues in the small intestine, aided by bile secreted by the liver and enzymes secreted by the pancreas. Most nutrients are absorbed into the bloodstream in the small intestine, through capillaries in the walls. The large intestine is responsible for absorbing water from body waste, compacting it, and storing it in the rectum for excretion.

Key Terms

Term	Definition
Absorption	The process in which digested food and nutrients are absorbed into the bloodstream through capillaries in the walls of the small intestine.
Amino acid	The basic building block of proteins.
Anus	The external opening where feces are excreted from the body.
Bile	Substance secreted by the liver and stored in the gall bladder; aids in the digestion of fat.
Canines	The longest teeth, which are located at the corners of incisors and are usually pointed at the tip. Canines are used to tear food.
Carbohydrate	One of the three main nutrients in food, along with fats and proteins. Simple carbohydrates come from fruit and sugars. Complex carbohydrates come from vegetables, rice, nuts, and grains. The body breaks carbohydrates down into glucose, a simple sugar used to feed cells.
Cecum	The first segment of the large intestine, where the absorption of nutrients is completed and waste products begin to be compacted.
Cellulose	The complex carbohydrate found in the cell walls of plants.
Chyme	A semi-fluid mixture of partially digested food and secretions which is produced in the stomach.
Colon	The second segment of the large intestine, where water is absorbed from body waste and compaction continues.

Key Terms

Term	Definition
Defecation	The process of excreting feces from the body.
Digestion	The process of breaking down food into simpler chemical compounds that are capable of being absorbed by the small intestine. Digestive processes are either mechanical (the chewing of food) or chemical (the chemical breakdown of food by enzymes).
Digestive enzyme	Substance that breaks the complex molecules of carbohydrates, fats, and proteins into simple building blocks that can be absorbed by the body.
Digestive system	The body system responsible for the digestion, or breakdown, of food so that nutrients can be absorbed into the bloodstream. The digestive system also eliminates solid waste products from the body.
Duodenum	The first segment of the small intestine, where secretions from the pancreas and gall bladder enter.
Fatty acid	The basic building block of fats.
Fats	A subgroup of lipids, which are formed when three fatty acids join with glycerol to form a molecule. Fats may be either saturated or unsaturated. Saturated fats are derived from animal sources and are known to raise blood cholesterol. Unsaturated fats are derived from plant and some animal sources, such as fish. A healthy diet includes eating foods that contain more unsaturated fats than saturated fats.
Ileum	The final segment of the small intestine. The absorption of nutrients begins in the jejunum of the small intestine and continues in the ileum.

Key Terms

Term	Definition
Incisors	Teeth located at the front of the mouth, which are used to grasp food.
Jejunum	The middle segment of the small intestine.
Lipids	Fat soluble molecules used for a variety of body processes.
Molars	Teeth with larger, flatter surfaces used by all species for grinding.
Premolars	Teeth located at the sides of the mouth; used to cut food.
Protein	Nutrient composed of amino acids, which is essential for the growth and repair of inner body tissues and skin, hair, and nails.
Rectum	The final part of the large intestine which stores feces for excretion by the body.
Ruminant	Animal that regurgitates swallowed food in order to rechew it, as part of the digestive process. Ruminant animals have four-chambered stomachs designed to ferment and digest large amounts of plant matter. They include cattle, sheep, and goats.

Answer key on page 199

What Do You Remember?

Exercise 7–1

1. _________ have the shortest digestive tracts, because meat is easily digested and takes little time.

a. Carnivores
b. Herbivores
c. Omnivores
d. Ruminants

2. _________ eat both meat and plant-based foods.

a. Carnivores
b. Herbivores
c. Omnivores
d. Ruminants

3. Mechanical digestion begins in the _____________.

a. stomach
b. small intestine
c. esophagus
d. oral cavity

4. Chemical digestion begins in the _______________.

a. stomach
b. small intestine
c. esophagus
d. oral cavity

Answer key on page 199

What Do You Remember?

5. Secretions from the pancreas and gall bladder enter the small intestine through the ____________.

a. jejunum
b. ileum
c. duodenum
d. cecum

6. The __________ secretes both digestive enzymes and insulin.

a. liver
b. gall bladder
c. pancreas
d. small intestine

7. Body waste is compacted in the ____________.

a. cecum
b. colon
c. rectum
d. both a and b

8. In ruminants, fiber from plant materials is broken down into fatty acids used for metabolic fuel in the ______________.

a. rumen
b. reticulum
c. omasum
d. abomasum

Answer key on page 199

What Do You Remember?

Exercise 7–2

Classify each of the foods listed below by the type of nutrient(s) they provide. For example, beef is a source of both fat and protein. Soybeans are a source of only protein.

1. soybeans
2. apples
3. peanut oil
4. sugar
5. potatoes
6. eggs
7. beef
8. honey
9. corn oil
10. wheat
11. rice
12. cheese
13. peas
14. chicken
15. milk

Simple Carbohydrate	Complex Carbohydrate	Complex Carbohydrate and Protein	Only Fat	Both Fat and Protein
		soybeans		beef

Pug

CHAPTER 8

The Urinary System

Highlights of the Chapter

- The organs of the urinary system and their function
- How urine is formed
- The urination process
- Urinalysis—the testing of urine samples

Introduction

The urinary system regulates the amount of water, minerals, and nutrients, as well as the acid balance, in the body. It also converts waste products into urine.

There are four major organs in an animal's urinary system:

- Kidneys
- Ureters
- The urinary bladder
- The urethra

Working together, these organs eliminate urea, salts, water, and other water-soluble waste products from the animal's body. The urinary system removes nearly all water-soluble waste products from blood and transports them out of the body.

The production of urine is vital to the body's health. As blood flows through the body, wastes resulting from the metabolism in cells are deposited into the bloodstream. This waste must be filtered out of the blood and disposed of.

A major part of this cleaning of the blood takes place in the kidneys. Normally about 20% of the total blood pumped by the heart each minute will enter the kidneys to be filtered. The remaining 80% flows through the rest of the body to meet nutritional, respiratory, and other needs the blood looks after.

This chapter will review the major parts of the urinary system and how they work. For more information about this topic, see *The Veterinary Assistant Career and Medical Terminology* (chapter 8, "Processing Nutrients and Waste").

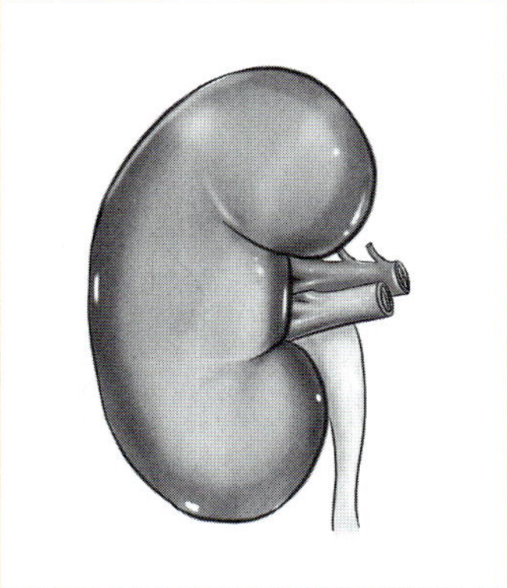

The Organs of the Urinary System

The Kidneys

The kidneys are responsible for filtering the blood, returning useful substances to the bloodstream, and removing waste products. The basic functional units of the kidney are called nephrons. Nephrons filter the blood and form urine. Each kidney contains hundreds of thousands of microscopic nephrons.

The body's waste products include urea, which is nitrogen waste from protein digestion. Urea is formed in the body to eliminate the toxic ammonia byproducts that are formed in the liver from amino acids. Since animals cannot excrete ammonia, these byproducts are converted to the less dangerous urea and then filtered out of the blood. Other waste products include salts and some medications that are removed from the blood by the kidneys.

Finally, the kidneys help maintain the acid-base balance in the blood by altering the excretion of either excess acid or bases from the body. This helps keep blood pH within normal levels.

The two kidneys (left and right) are bean-shaped and are located in the abdominal cavity. They lie on either side of the vertebral column between the first and third lumbar vertebrae. The renal artery supplies the kidneys with blood. The renal vein drains filtered blood from the kidneys.

Each kidney has three regions:

- The renal cortex (which contains the nephrons)
- The renal medulla
- The renal pelvis

Figure 8.1 Parts of a Kidney

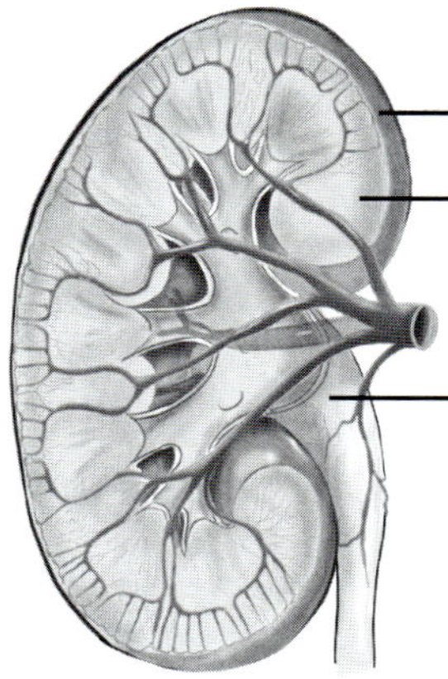

The Ureters

The ureters are tubes that use muscle contractions to continuously move urine from the kidneys to the urinary bladder. The right ureter is connected to the right kidney. The left ureter is connected to the left kidney.

While the bladder is filling, the ureters stay open, allowing urine to flow freely into the bladder. When the bladder is full, the pressure of the urine collapses the ureters' openings, preventing urine from flowing back into them after it is expelled. It doesn't prevent more urine from entering the bladder, because the ureters' contractions are strong enough to push through the collapsed openings into the bladder.

The Urinary Bladder

The urinary bladder stores urine as it is produced and releases it during urination. The bladder has two parts: a muscular sac and a neck. The urinary bladder looks and functions much like a balloon. Both the bladder sac size and its position will vary depending on the amount of urine it contains. The tissues lining the bladder will stretch as it fills with urine, like filling a balloon with water. The wall of the bladder contains smooth muscles. When these contract, the bladder is squeezed and urine is expelled, like letting water out of a balloon.

The neck of the bladder extends downward into the pelvis and connects to the urethra. The contraction and relaxation of sphincter muscles in the neck open and close the passageway for urine to enter the urethra.

The Urethra

The urethra carries urine from the urinary bladder to the external environment. Its anatomy and location is different in males and females. In female animals, it is short and straight. In male animals, it is longer and curved. In females, the urethra opens into the ventral floor of the reproductive tract, at a point known as the external urethral orifice. In males, it runs down the center of the penis.

How Urine Is Formed

Urine is 95% water and 5% waste products, such as salts and urea. It is formed in the kidneys before being released by the body.

Three processes occur in the kidneys to form urine:

- Filtration
- Reabsorption
- Secretion

Glomerular filtration, the first process of urine formation, occurs in the nephrons. The nephrons contain a cluster of capillaries called the glomerulus. First, blood enters the kidneys through the renal artery. As the blood flows through the glomerular walls and into a membrane known as Bowman's capsule, water, sugar, salts and waste products are filtered out of the blood.

In the second process, tubular reabsorption, occurs as the filtered products travel through long, coiled tubes called renal tubules. Water, sugar, and salts are returned to the bloodstream through capillaries surrounding the tubules. This process prevents substances needed by the body from being lost in the urine.

Most of the water that leaves the bloodstream during filtration gets reabsorbed during this stage. In healthy patients, all of the glucose is also entirely reabsorbed back into the blood. But if too much glucose is present, the tubules reach the limit of their ability to return sugar to the bloodstream. The excess glucose is carried along in the urine, providing a veterinarian with his or her first clue that a patient has diabetes.

Sodium ions, or salts, are only partially reabsorbed from the renal tubules back into the blood. Some salts are excreted in the urine. How much salt is excreted in urine will depend on an animal's salt intake. As salt intake increases, the kidneys decrease the amount of sodium reabsorption back into the blood. The reverse is true when salt intake decreases.

In the third and final process, tubular secretion, waste substances are transferred from the blood into the renal tubules, where they mix with water and are converted into urine. The urine is transported through the renal tubules into the renal pelvis.

Secretion is the opposite of absorption. Whereas absorption moves substances out of the tubules and into the blood, secretion moves substances out of the blood and into the tubules to form urine.

Figure 8.2 The Brain Signaling the Bladder

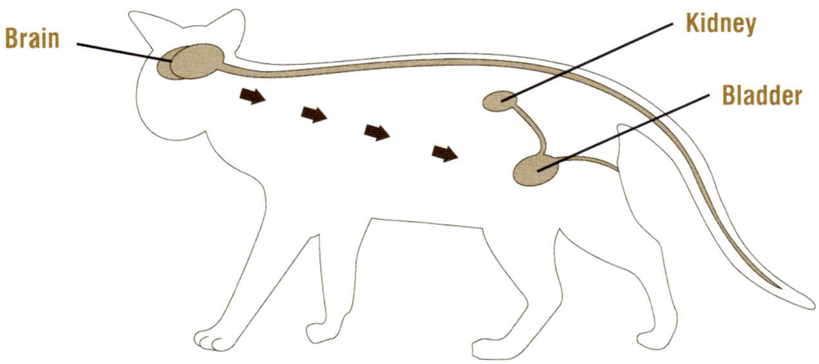

The Urination Process

When the bladder is full, a nerve impulse is sent to the muscles in the bladder wall to contract. These contractions create the sensation of having to urinate. Urine leaves the body through the urethra. This process is called urination, or voiding.

Dogs and other animals that have been trained can control the reflex release of urine through voluntary control of the bladder's sphincter muscle. But there is a limit to how long an animal can hold urine in its bladder. As the bladder gets fuller, it puts more pressure on the sphincter muscle, eventually causing it to relax and release urine. This is when "accidents" happen. Do not expect animals to hold their urine for long periods, and provide dogs with frequent opportunities to void outside.

The amount of urine produced helps ensure that the body contains the right amount of water to maintain a healthy internal environment. If the body has excess water it needs to get rid of, more urine is formed and excreted. If the body needs to conserve water, less urine is formed and excreted, or none at all.

Urinalysis

Urinalysis is the laboratory examination and evaluation of a urine sample. It involves a visual examination of the sample for color and clarity, as well as a microscopic and chemical evaluation.

Normal urine can range in color from light yellow to amber, depending mostly on the level of hydration in the body. Dark yellow urine usually indicates dehydration. Drugs and some diseases may also alter the color of urine. Normal urine is also transparent or clear. Substances that can cause urine to be cloudy include white or red blood cells, crystals, mucus, fat, and bacteria.

Urinalysis helps veterinarians to diagnose medical conditions. It provides a lot of useful information about how well an animal's urinary system is working and the patient's health in general. For example, the presence of fresh blood may be caused by trauma of the urinary tract or a bladder infection. Glucose in the urine may indicate diabetes. Bile may indicate liver disease or blockage of the bile duct.

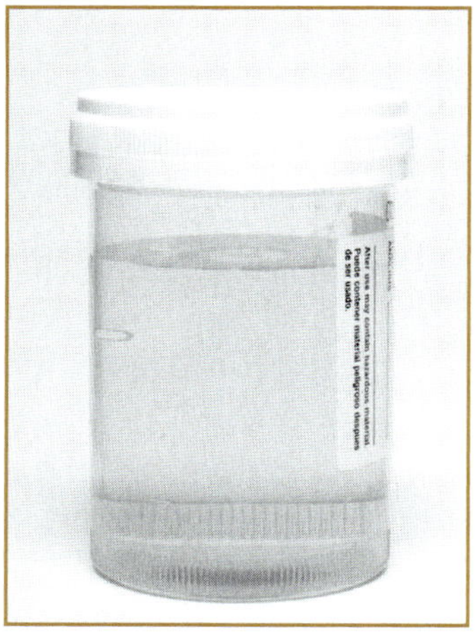

Summary

The urinary system's major function is to regulate the amount of water, minerals, and nutrients, as well as the acid balance in the body. It also converts waste products into urine, the liquid form of waste in the body.

An animal's urinary system comprises the following:

- Kidneys, which remove waste products from blood
- Ureters, which are long, narrow muscular tubes that connect each kidney to the bladder
- The urinary bladder, which is the storage reservoir for urine, found in the lower abdomen
- The urethra, which is a small tube that leads from the bladder out of the animal's body

Urine is formed through the following three processes:

- Filtration of water and dissolved substances out of the blood in the glomerulus and into Bowman's capsule
- Reabsorption of water and dissolved substances out of renal tubules back into the blood
- Secretion of salts, urea, and some drugs out of the blood and into the renal tubules, where they are eventually eliminated in the urine

Normal urine is 95% water and 5% waste products, such as salts and urea. Urinalysis helps veterinarians to diagnose medical conditions. It provides a lot of useful information about how well an animal's urinary system is working and the patient's health in general.

Key Terms

Term	Definition
Glomerular filtration	Filtration of water and dissolved substances out of the blood in the glomerulus and into Bowman's capsule.
Kidneys	Double organs that filter and remove waste products from blood.
Nephrons	The blood-filtering mechanisms in kidneys that form urine.
Renal cortex	The outer region of the kidney that contains nephrons.
Renal medulla	The inner region of the kidney that contains the renal tubules.
Renal pelvis	The part of the kidney that forms the beginning of the ureters and brings urine collected by the renal tubules to them.
Renal tubules	Long, coiled tubes in the kidneys that collect urine.
Tubular reabsorption	Reabsorption of water and dissolved substances out of renal tubules in the kidneys back into the blood.
Tubular secretion	Secretion of salts, urea, and some drugs out of the blood and into the renal tubules of the kidneys, where they are eventually eliminated in the urine.
Urea	One of the end products of protein metabolism which is excreted from the body in urine.
Ureters	Long, narrow muscular tubes that connect each kidney to the bladder.
Urethra	The small tube that leads from the bladder out of the animal's body.

Key Terms

Term	Definition
Urinary bladder	The storage reservoir for urine, found in the lower abdomen.
Urinary system	The body system that regulates the amount of water, minerals, and nutrients, as well as the acid balance in the body. It also converts waste products into urine.
Urine	The liquid form of waste in the body.

Answer key on page 199

What Do You Remember?

Match the parts of the urinary system with their descriptions listed below.

1. kidneys	a. the outer region of the kidney that contains nephrons
2. nephrons	b. the storage organ for urine
3. renal cortex	c. the inner region of the kidney that contains the renal tubules
4. renal medulla	d. tube that lead from the bladder out of the body
5. renal pelvis	e. tubes in the kidney that collect urine
6. renal tubules	f. double organs that filter and remove waste products from blood
7. ureters	g. blood-filtering mechanisms in the kidneys that form urine
8. urethra	h. the part of the kidney that connects to the ureters
9. urinary bladder	i. long tubes that connect the kidneys to the bladder

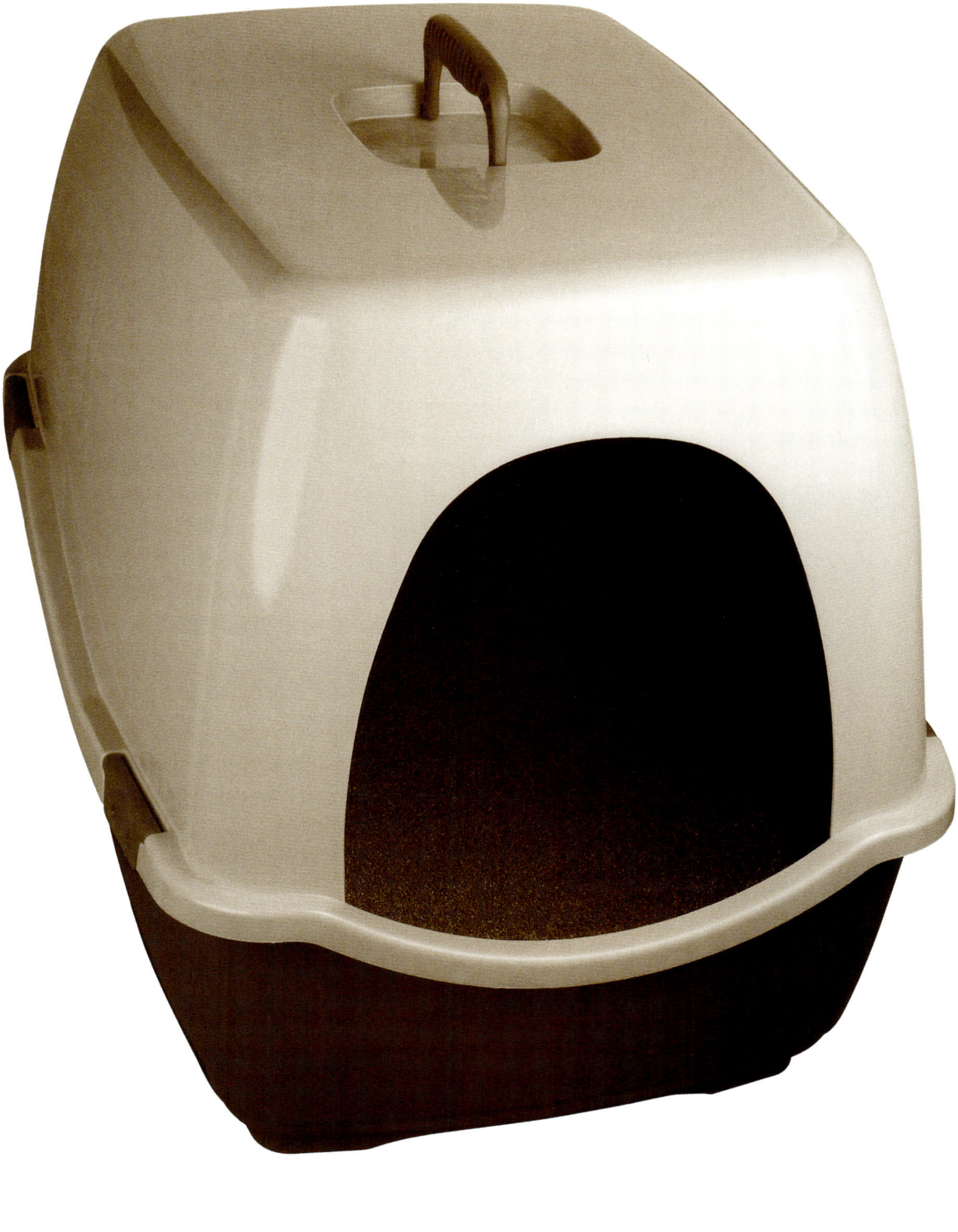

Cat Litter Box

Golden Retriever Puppies

CHAPTER 9

The Reproductive System

Highlights of the Chapter

- The anatomical parts and processes related to domestic animals' reproductive systems
- The reproductive cycles of females
- Fertilization of ovum
- Pregnancy and the birthing process
- Lactation

Introduction

Unlike other body systems that work to ensure an individual animal's survival, the reproductive system exists to ensure the survival of an entire animal species. The male reproductive system produces, transports, and delivers sperm, which fertilizes the ovum (egg cell) produced by the female.

Male and female domestic animals have very different reproductive systems, both internally and externally. In the female animal, the reproductive system is found in both the abdominal and pelvic cavities. In the male, it lies in the pelvic cavity.

This chapter will summarize the parts and processes related to domestic animals' reproductive systems. For a more detailed discussion, see *The Veterinary Assistant Career and Medical Terminology* (chapter 11, "Survival of the Species").

The Male Reproductive System

Domestic male animals have two testicles, which produce male sex hormones (the most important of which is testosterone) and the male sex cell, sperm. Sperm are constantly being produced in very large numbers to help ensure that one will reach and fertilize the ovum when breeding occurs.

The testicles are contained in a pouch of skin called the scrotum, where they are protected and supported. The scrotum also keeps the testicles cooler than the rest of the body, because the ideal temperature for sperm production is about 2 to 3°C lower than body temperature.

The spermatic cords link the testes with the rest of the body. They are tube-like connective tissue structures that contain blood vessels, nerves, lymphatic vessels, and the vas deferens. The vas deferens are two muscular tubes that propel sperm and the fluid in which they are suspended from their storage site in the testes to the urethra, where ejaculation occurs.

Reproductive organs in male domestic animals also include the prostate gland, the urethra, the penis, and the prepuce.

Figure 9.1 Male Reproductive System

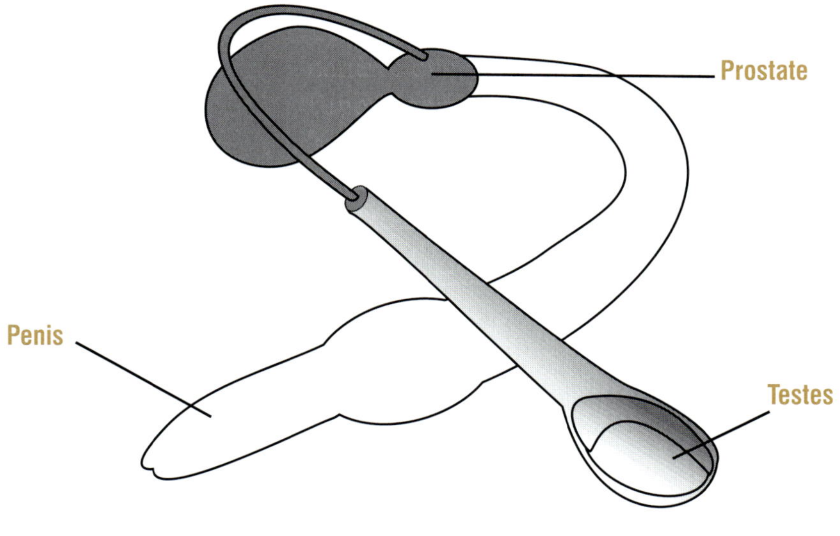

The Female Reproductive System

Female animals have two ovaries that both contain ova (eggs). The ovaries also produce both estrogens and progestins. Estrogens create the physical and behavioral changes that prepare females for breeding and pregnancy. Progestins, such as progesterone, help prepare the uterus for implantation of a fertilized ovum. They are also necessary for pregnancy to be maintained.

Ova are not produced continuously like sperm. At birth, a female animal has a fixed number of immature ova formed in her ovaries. That is the total number available to her in her lifetime. Each ovarian cycle produces one or more mature ova, depending on the species. Each cycle includes the development of an ovum within a follicle and its release from the follicle, called ovulation.

The number of ova produced per cycle depends on the species involved. Cattle and horses, who give birth to only one offspring at a time, release one mature ovum per cycle. Cats, dogs, and sows, which give birth to litters of young, produce multiple ova per cycle.

During ovulation, ova travel down the uterine tube and are deposited into the fallopian tubes, where they are fertilized by spermatozoa. The fallopian tubes then guide fertilized ova from the ovary to the uterus.

Figure 9.2 Female Reproductive System

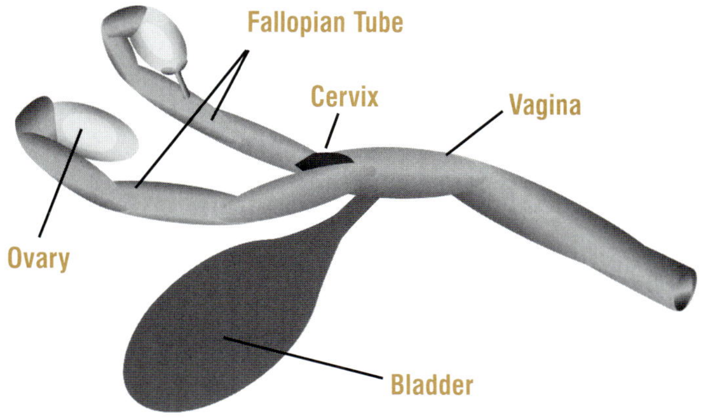

After ovulation, a hormone-producing structure called the corpus luteum develops in the ovaries. It produces several progestins, the most important of which is progesterone. Progesterone helps prepare the uterus to receive the fertilized ovum. The hormone also maintains pregnancy once the fertilized ovum is implanted in the uterus.

The uterus is the womb, where the fertilized ovum implants and lives while it develops into a fetus. The uterus has several parts: a neck (or cervix), a body, and the two uterine horns.

The cervix is a thick-walled structure through which the cervical canal runs. Sperm passes into the uterus through the cervical canal, which also dilates to allow fetuses into the birth canal during the birthing process.

The vagina is a passageway for both the reproductive and urinary tracts and serves as a birth canal. The vaginal opening is called the vulva.

The female reproductive system also includes the mammary glands, which are located just under the skin on the ventral wall of the abdomen and thorax. Mammary glands produce milk after an animal has given birth.

The Reproductive Cycle of Females

The period during which female mammals ovulate and go into heat is called estrus, and this is the only time during which the female is able to conceive. Because ovum production in the ovary is cyclical rather than continuous, the timing of breeding is controlled by the female's ovarian cycle. This is when the chance of a successful pregnancy is highest.

The time from the beginning of one heat period to the beginning of the next is called the estrous cycle. The number of estrous cycles a female animal has each year depends on the species. For example, the female dog usually has two breeding seasons a year. Other species, such as the cat and rabbit, have a long breeding season during the spring and summer months. In some species, such as cats, ferrets, and rabbits, ovulation does not occur until the females have been bred. These species are called induced ovulators. If they are not bred, they remain in a prolonged state of heat.

Fertilization of Ovum

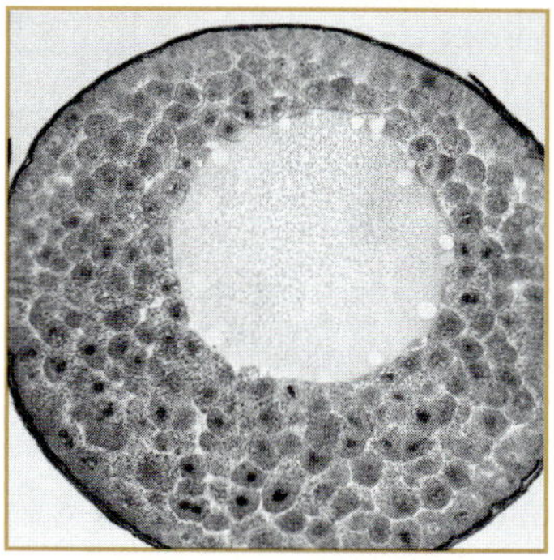

During ejaculation, semen is expelled from the penis into the female reproductive tract. Contractions of the uterus transport active sperm upward to the fallopian tubes, where the mature ovum or ova are waiting to be fertilized.

An ovum becomes fertilized when one sperm penetrates through the cell membrane to deliver its genetic material into the cell. A fertilized ovum is called a zygote, which contains a full set of chromosomes, half of them from each of the two sex cells that produced it.

The zygote begins to divide rapidly through mitosis. Mitosis is the process in which a cell's nucleus replicates and divides in preparation for division of the cell. The single cell divides into two identical cells, then four, then eight, then 16, and so on. While mitosis is taking place, the zygote is slowly moving down the fallopian tube toward the uterus. Muscular contractions and hair-like projections called cilia help propel it.

Implantation occurs when the zygote attaches itself to the uterine lining.

Pregnancy

Pregnancy, or gestation, is when the female is carrying young in the uterus. The gestation period is the time from fertilization of the ovum to delivery of the newborn.

During pregnancy, the offspring's cells differentiate into all of the tissues, organs, and body systems that will be needed to support independent life after birth.

There are two phases of gestation:

- The embryonic stage
- The fetal stage

As the embryo/fetus develops, the placenta forms around it and attaches to the uterine lining so that nutrients, wastes, and respiratory gases can be exchanged between the fetal and maternal bloodstreams. The placenta is the life-support system that keeps the fetus alive during pregnancy.

The placenta is connected to the fetus by the umbilical cord. All blood and nutrients pass from the mother through the placenta to the developing embryo/fetus. The placenta forms a sac around the fetus called the amniotic sac. The fetus floats in amniotic fluid inside this sac.

Table 9.1 shows the length of gestation periods for various domestic animal species and the average number of young they have.

The Birthing Process

Table 9.1 Gestation Periods and Average Number of Young of Domestic Animals

Species	Gestation Period (Days)	Average Number of Young
Cattle	280–290	1
Cats	60–65	8–10
Dogs	60–65	8–10
Goats	145–155	1–3
Horses	330–340	1
Pigs	110–115	6–12
Sheep	140–150	1–2

The birthing process is call parturition, or labor, and its onset is signaled by hormonal changes. There are three stages of parturition. During the first stage, contractions of the uterus begin and the cervix dilates to make room for the fetus.

During the second stage of labor, strong uterine and abdominal muscle contractions push the young through the birth canal and the offspring are born. These contractions push the fetus from the uterine horn, through the uterine body, and into the vagina. Continued contractions push the fetus from the female's body. Rupture of the amniotic sac usually happens before the newborn is delivered.

In the third stage of labor, the placenta separates from the uterine wall and is expelled from the body. Uterine contractions will continue to expel the placenta, which is referred to as the "afterbirth."

When a female animal is giving birth to a litter, the second and third stages of labor will intermix. Typically, after a newborn is delivered, its placenta is expelled before the next newborn is delivered.

A newborn animal is called a neonate. Immediately after being born, the neonate's lungs must expand and start functioning to provide it with the oxygen it needs to survive.

Lactation

The secretion of milk from the mammary glands to feed neonates is called lactation. The process occurs in all female mammals and is usually stimulated by hormones. Once it has begun, lactation will continue with regular nursing or milking. When nursing or milking stops, so too does the flow of hormones that causes lactation to occur. Eventually, the mammary glands cease producing milk.

Colostrum is the first milk produced by the mammary glands. It contains larger amounts of nutrients and essential vitamins than regular milk. It also contains antibodies that transfer passive immunity from mothers to their offspring. This helps to protect neonates from disease until their own immune systems develop. It is very important that neonates consume colostrum during the first few hours after being born, because this is the only time maternal antibodies can be absorbed by its bloodstream. Neonates that do not consume colostrum are more prone to disease and do not thrive as well as those that do.

Summary

Mammals reproduce through sexual reproduction. Their offspring are the result of the random combination of the genes of the two parents. Offspring are genetically different from their parents and each other. This is how genetic variation occurs in mammals.

The male reproductive system produces, transports, and delivers sperm, which fertilizes the ovum (egg cell) produced by the female. The female reproductive system's main function is reproduction, the process of producing offspring. The ovaries produce female sex cells (ova) and hormones, whereas the testes produce male sex cells (sperm) and hormones.

During pregnancy, the offspring's cells differentiate into all of the tissues, organs, and body systems that will be needed to support independent life after birth. There are two phases of gestation: the embryonic stage and the fetal stage. The embryonic stage lasts from fertilization of the ovum until all of the organs are formed. The embryo then becomes a fetus, which has the main recognizable features of a mature animal. The fetal stage lasts until birth.

Key Terms

Term	Definition
Cervix	The structure between the uterus and the vagina.
Embryo	The embryonic stage lasts from fertilization of the ovum until all of the organs are formed. The embryo then becomes a fetus, which has the main recognizable features of a mature animal.
Endometrium	The lining of the uterus, which consists of epithelial cells, gland tissue, and blood capillaries.
Estrous cycle	The period during which female mammals ovulate and are in heat.
Fetus	A growing embryo becomes a fetus once all of the organs are formed. The fetal stage then lasts until birth.
Induced ovulators	Animal species in which ovulation does not occur until the females have been bred. Cats, ferrets, and rabbits are all induced ovulators.
Lactation	The secretion of milk from the mammary glands to feed neonates after birth.
Mammary glands	Glands that produce milk after an animal has given birth. Female dogs have five pairs of mammary glands, and female cats have four pairs.
Mitosis	The process in which a cell's nucleus replicates and divides in preparation for division of the cell.
Neonate	A newborn animal.
Ovum	The female sex cell. The plural form of ovum is ova.
Ovary	Female animals have a pair of ovaries that both contain ova. Ovaries also produce female sex hormones.

Key Terms

Term	Definition
Ovulation	The process by which ova are released from the ovaries.
Penis	The male reproductive organ that delivers spermatozoa during mating.
Placenta	The organ that feeds and nourishes the embryo/fetus, while also disposing of waste. All blood and nutrients pass from the mother through the placenta to the developing embryo/fetus.
Prostate gland	The gland that secretes seminal fluid.
Spermatozoa/sperm	The male sex cell.
Testes/testicles	Domestic male animals have two testes, or testicles, which produce spermatozoa and male sex hormones.
Uterine horns	The uterus of female domestic animals, such as dogs and cats, is divided into two horns to facilitate carriage of multiple fetuses during gestation.
Uterus	The female reproductive organ where the embryo/fetus develops.
Vagina	The passageway for both the reproductive and urinary tracts, which serves as a birth canal.
Zygote	A fertilized ovum that contains a full set of chromosomes, half of them from each of the two sex cells that produced it.

Answer key on page 199

What Do You Remember?

1. In the male, sperm are produced by the ________.

a. scrotum
b. testes
c. vas deferens
d. prostate gland

2. Seminal fluid is produced by the ___________.

a. scrotum
b. testes
c. vas deferens
d. prostate gland

3. In the female, ova are fertilized by sperm in the _______________.

a. fallopian tubes
b. ovaries
c. uterus
d. uterine horns

4. Once it has implanted in the uterus, a fertilized ovum becomes a/an _____________.

a. zygote
b. neonate
c. fetus
d. embryo

Answer key on page 199

What Do You Remember?

5. **____________ is another word for pregnancy.**

a. Parturition
b. Gestation
c. Fertilization
d. Ovulation

6. **____________ is another word for giving birth.**

a. Parturition
b. Gestation
c. Fertilization
d. Ovulation

7. **The ____________ is the life-support system that supplies nutrients to the fetus.**

a. uterus
b. amniotic sac
c. placenta
d. endometrium

8. **Which of the following species are induced ovulators?**

a. rabbits
b. cats
c. cattle
d. both a and b

Filly

Crocodile

CHAPTER 10

The Nervous and Sensory Systems

Highlights of the Chapter

- Structures of the nervous system
- The parts of the brain and their functions
- How animals experience pain
- Organs of the sensory system and their functions

Introduction

The nervous system comprises the brain, spinal column, and peripheral nerves. The nervous system enables an animal to receive, interpret, and respond to stimuli. It is responsible for regulating and controlling body functions, controlling consciousness, processing sensory information, and transmitting motor impulses from the brain to the body.

Within the nervous system, electrical signals are transmitted at very high speed along nerve fibers. This provides a means of communication between various parts of the body, which is essential for an animal's survival.

The nervous system senses changes both from within the body and in the external environment. It responds by sending sensory information to the brain and spinal cord which is analyzed and integrated to produce a motor response. For example, the motor response in an animal fleeing from a perceived threat would likely involve contracting muscles to move the body and releasing sweat from sweat glands.

The sensory system includes the sensory organs (eyes, ears, mouth, nose, skin) as well as sensory areas of the brain. An animal's sensory organs allow it to perceive and interact with its environment.

The Nervous System

The basic unit of the nervous system is the neuron, which receives and transmits nerve impulses throughout the body. They are the core components of the brain, the spinal cord, and the peripheral nerves.

There are three main types of neurons:

- Sensory neurons respond to touch, sound, light, and other stimuli affecting sensory organs. They also send sensory signals to the spinal cord and brain.
- Motor neurons receive signals from the brain and spinal cord. They also cause muscle contractions and activity within glands.
- Interneurons connect neurons to other neurons within the brain and spinal cord.

Figure 10.1 The Nervous System

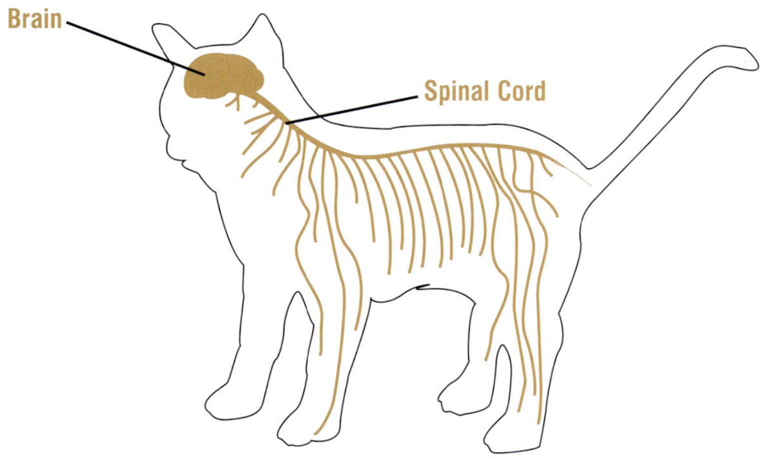

Figure 10.2 Subsystems of the Nervous System

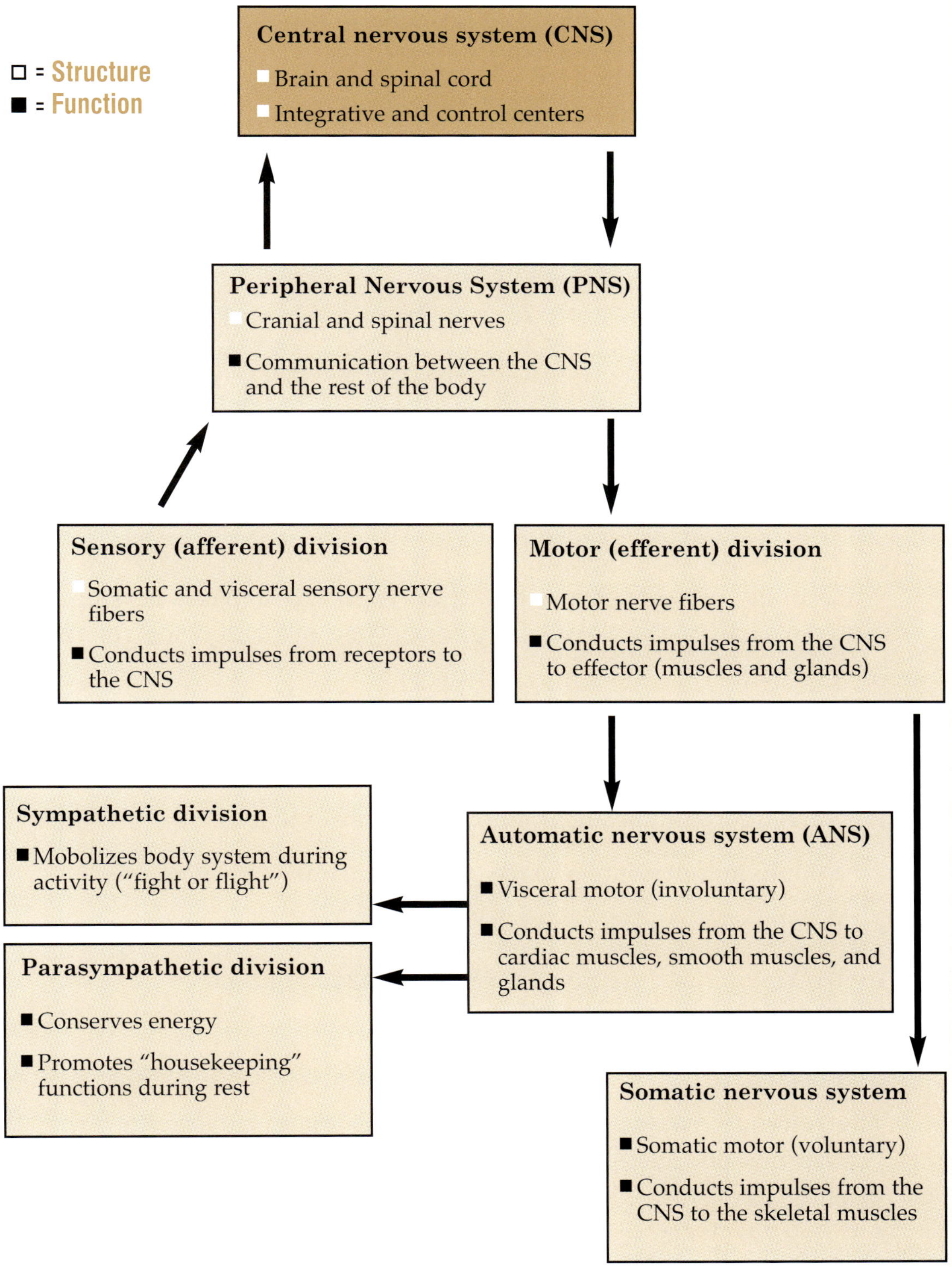

Each neuron has a cell body, an axon, and many dendrites. Information is received from other neurons by the dendrites, which are short branches of the cell body. Information is transmitted to other neurons down the axon.

Figure 10.3 Neurons

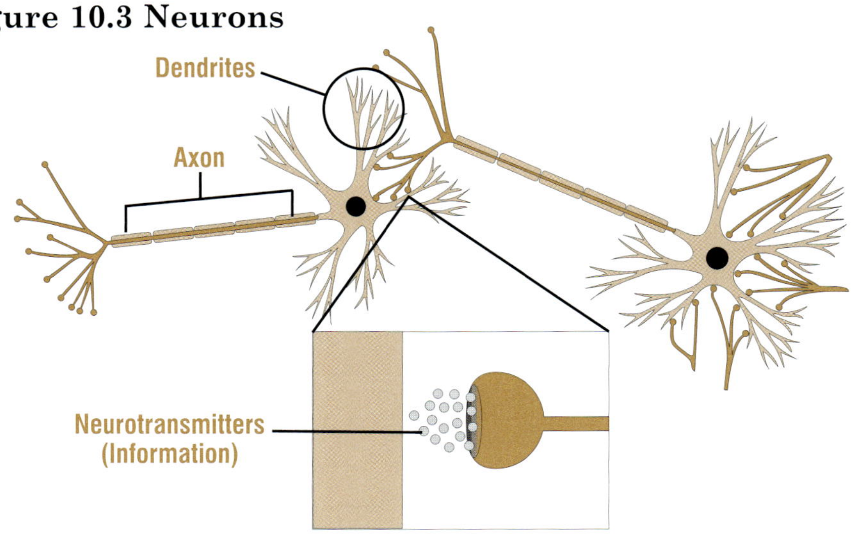

Glial cells are non-neuronal cells that participate in signal transmission in the nervous system. They are the "glue" of the nervous system.

There are four main functions of glial cells:

- Surrounding neurons and holding them in place
- Supplying nutrients and oxygen to neurons
- Insulating neurons from each other
- Destroying pathogens and removing dead neurons

Subsystems

The nervous system is divided into two main subsystems: the central nervous system and the peripheral nervous system.

The central nervous system is composed of the brain and spinal cord, which, together, control the peripheral nervous system, which includes the collective nervous structures found outside of the central nervous system. The central nervous system is protected the skull and the vertebral column, as well as by cerebral spinal fluid, which flows throughout the brain and spinal cord to cushion organs from injury, and the meninges, a three-layered membrane.

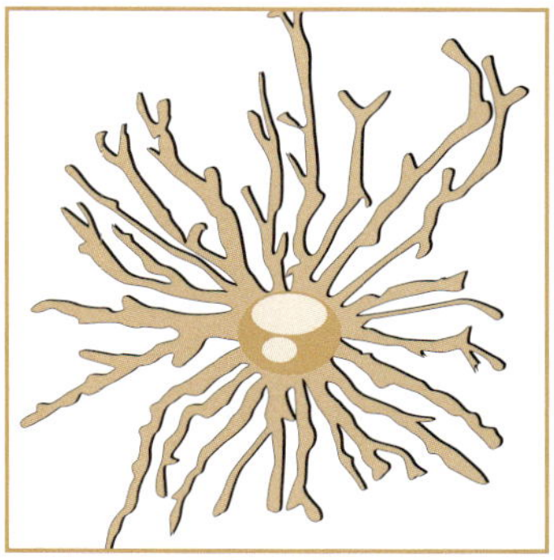

The peripheral nervous system is composed of nerves that transmit motor messages from and sensory messages to the brain and spinal cord. The peripheral nerves connected to the brain are called cranial nerves; the peripheral nerves connected to the spinal cord are called spinal nerves.

The cranial nerves carry information between the brain and the sensory organs. They also relay nerve impulses related to sensations in facial skin and the motor control of muscles in the face, scalp, jaw, tongue, neck, and shoulder. Cranial nerves may be sensory, motor, or a combination of both.

The spinal nerves relay sensory and motor information between the brain and the limbs and lower parts of the body. Between each pair of vertebrae, the spinal cord contains dorsal and ventral nerve roots from each side that combine to form the left and right spinal nerves. Sensory information comes into the spinal cord via the dorsal nerve roots. Motor instructions are sent to various parts of the body via the ventral nerve roots.

The peripheral nervous system is divided into the automatic, or autonomic, nervous system and the somatic nervous system. The automatic nervous system is responsible for controlling involuntary actions and responses. It supplies nerves to all of the body's internal organs. It is responsible for controlling and regulating automatic processes related to essential body functions, such as heart rate, blood pressure, body temperature, respiration, and digestion. Automatic motor nerves send impulses to smooth muscles contained in organs, cardiac muscle, and glands to regulate the body's many automatic processes.

The automatic nervous system is subdivided into the sympathetic and parasympathetic nervous systems. These two systems have opposite effects on organs and body tissues. The sympathetic nervous system is often called the "fight-or-flight" system, because it helps an animal to either defend itself (fight) or escape (flight) in an emergency.

The sympathetic nervous system also helps to maintain blood pressure when an animal has lost a significant amount of blood, is very dehydrated, or is in shock. It does so by increasing heart rate and constricting arterioles (small blood vessels) in the skin and body systems. These two actions result in more blood being directed to the brain in an attempt to ensure the brain continues to receive adequate blood flow.

The parasympathetic nervous system is also called the "rest-and-restore" system because it brings the body back to a resting state after the emergency is over. The parasympathetic nervous system causes heart and breathing rates, as well as blood pressure, to return to normal. It also helps the body to conserve energy when it is at rest.

The somatic nervous system controls movement of the muscles. It is usually under voluntary control. Impulses sent to the central nervous system from receptors in the muscles, skin, eyes, ears, nose, and tongue are all somatic sensory functions because they are consciously perceived by the brain. The only exceptions are when an animal is unconscious or during a reflex response, such as when an animal withdraws a limb from a sharp object to avoid pain.

The Brain

The brain interprets and coordinates most stimuli. It can be thought of as the central supercomputer of the body.

The brain is composed of billions of neurons that communicate with each other through neurotransmitters. In the brain, many neurons are interconnected to form neural networks. A neuron may be connected to a thousand or more other neurons. Neural networks are the basis of perception, behavior, different types of action, and cognitive function.

The largest part of the brain is called the cerebrum. It is believed to control learning, emotions, and behavior in animals. It has right and left hemispheres. The corpus callosum connects the two hemispheres of the brain and maintains the flow of information between them.

Figure 10.4 Brain of a Domestic Animal

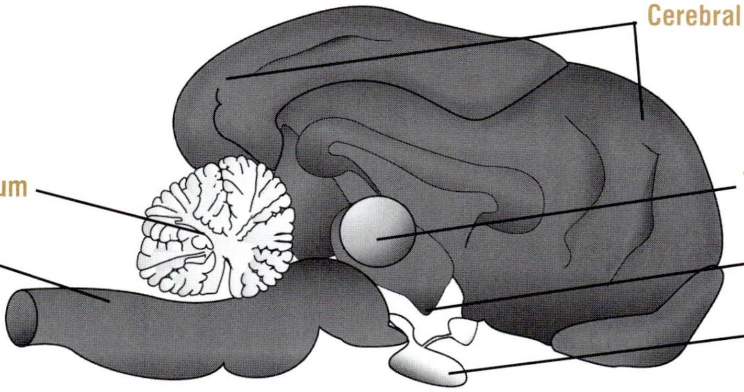

The cerebrum includes the cerebral cortex, the outer layer of the brain. It integrates neuron activity related to communication, emotional response, learning, memory, recall, and other conscious behaviors.

Located beneath the cerebrum, the cerebellum is the second largest section of the brain. It maintains balance and posture, and coordinates movement. It helps make movements smooth and accurate by comparing the movement the brain intends with the body's actual position and stimulating muscles to fine-tune the movement. It also helps maintain equilibrium and balance by receiving information from structures in the inner ear, as well as visual and tactile input.

The diencephalon serves as the passageway between the brain stem and the cerebrum. Its common name is "between brain." The major structures in the diencephalon are the thalamus, the hypothalamus, and the pituitary gland.

The thalamus receives information from the senses and sends that information to the cerebral cortex, the part of the cerebrum that processes sensory information. Stimuli related to the sense of smell are coordinated separately. The olfactory bulb beneath the cerebrum sends information related to the sense of smell from the nose to the brain.

The hypothalamus lies beneath the thalamus. Its main job is to preserve homeostasis. It regulates body temperature, appetite, thirst, digestion, water balance, and sleeping and waking cycles. Below the hypothalamus lies the pituitary gland. It is part of the endocrine system and secretes a wide range of hormones. The pituitary is often described as the "master gland" because it affects the actions of many other glands and forms a link with the nervous system.

The brainstem attaches the brain to the spinal cord. Its name comes from its appearance as a stem on which other parts of the brain sit. The brainstem maintains many of the body's basic support functions, and many of the cranial nerves originate from it.

It has three parts:

- The midbrain
- The pons
- The medulla oblongata

Figure 10.5 Brainstem

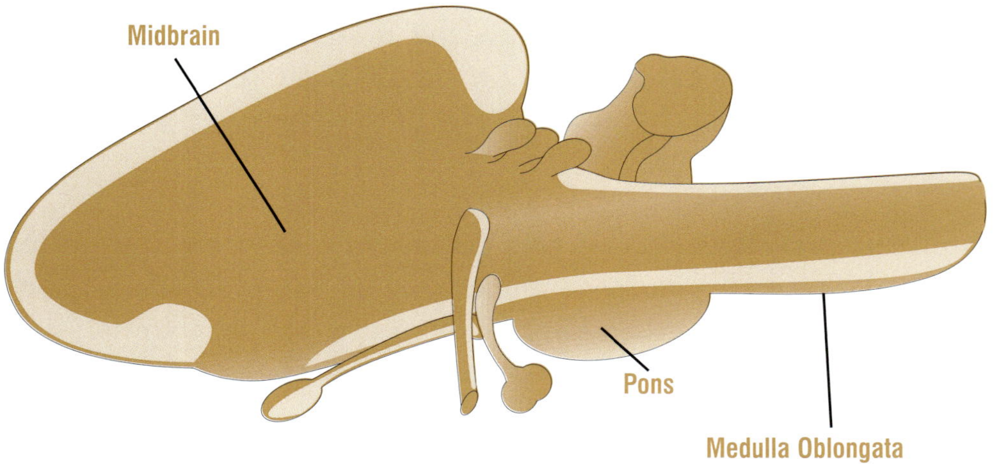

The nervous system interacts with all other body systems and controls organs within those systems directly. The brain also receives information from many organs and adjusts its signals to these organs to maintain proper functioning. Table 10.2 summarizes the interactions between the nervous system and other body systems.

The Blood-Brain Barrier

The blood-brain barrier is a functional barrier separating the brain's capillaries from its nervous tissue. Other capillaries in the body have small openings between the cells of their walls. The brain's capillaries are aligned tightly together without these openings and are covered by the cell membranes of glial cells. This tightly built capillary wall prevents many drugs, proteins, and other molecules from passing from the blood into the brain. It protects the brain from many poisons circulating in the bloodstream.

Table 10.1 Brain Structures and Their Functions

Brain Structure	Function
Cerebral cortex	Thought Voluntary movement Communication Learning Perception Emotional response
Cerebellum	Movement Balance Posture
Brain stem	Breathing Heart rate Blood pressure
Hypothalamus	Body temperature Hunger, thirst, and digestion Circadian rhythms Water balance
Thalamus	Sensory processing
Midbrain	Eye movements Arousal Respiration Cardiac functions

Table 10.2 How the Nervous System Interacts with Other Body Systems

Body System	Interaction with the Nervous System
Skeletal	Bones provide calcium, which is essential for proper functioning of the nervous system The skull protects the brain from injury The vertebrae protect the spinal cord from injury Sensory receptors in joints send signals about body position to the brain The brain moves bones by contracting muscles
Cardiovascular	The brain regulates heart rate and blood pressure
Muscular	Receptors in muscles provide the brain with information about body position and movement The brain controls muscle contractions
Endocrine	Hormones provide feedback to the brain to affect neural processing The hypothalamus controls the pituitary gland and other endocrine glands
Lymphatic	The brain stimulates the lymphatic system's defense mechanisms against infection
Respiratory	The brain monitors respiratory rate, respiratory volume, and levels of oxygen and carbon dioxide in the blood
Digestive	The digestive system sends sensory information to the brain The automatic nervous system controls the involuntary movement of muscles in digestive organs while food is being digested The brain controls drinking and feeding behavior, as well as the muscles used for eating and elimination of solid waste
Reproductive	Reproductive hormones affect brain development and sexual behavior The brain controls mating behavior
Urinary	The bladder sends sensory information to the brain The brain controls urination
Integumentary (skin and accessory structures: hair, claws, hooves, and horns)	Receptors in the skin send sensory information to the brain The automatic nervous system regulates blood flow to the skin and sweat gland activity Nerves control muscles connected to hair follicles

Pain Receptors

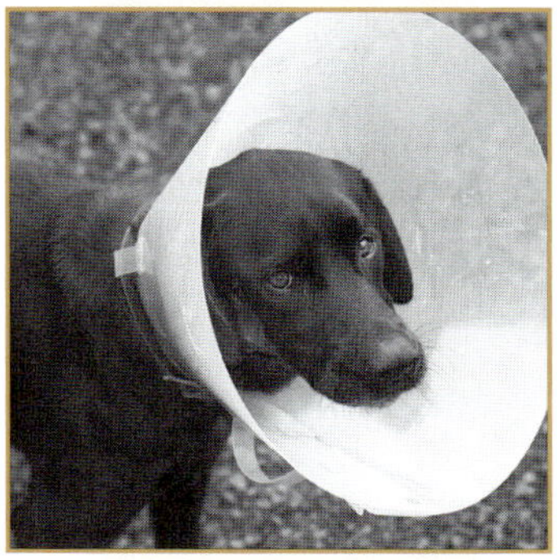

Pain receptors are widely distributed throughout the body, both on the surface and internally. Their purpose is to protect the body from damage by alerting the central nervous system to potentially harmful stimuli. The only place in the body where pain receptors are not found is the brain.

Pain may be the result of either mechanical, chemical, or thermal stimuli. Four steps have to occur before animals or people feel pain. First, the painful stimulus is converted to a nerve impulse at the sensory nerve ending. Second, the impulse travels to the spinal cord. Next, the spinal cord modulates the nerve impulse and may either amplify or suppress it, depending on the severity of the pain. Finally, several areas of the brain, including the cerebral cortex, perceive the painful impulse.

Depending on where it occurs in the body, pain may be classified into three categories:

- Superficial, affecting the skin
- Deep, affecting muscles and joints
- Visceral, affecting internal organs

It may also be classified as acute (sharp and intense) or chronic (dull and aching).

Unlike people, animals tend to hide signs that they are in pain. This is a survival instinct. An animal that shows signs of pain is showing signs of weakness that might encourage predators to attack it. Visible reactions to pain vary greatly among species, breeds, and individual animals. Some animals appear to be highly sensitive to mild pain, whereas others don't react until pain becomes severe.

Analgesia is a state in which the perception of pain is decreased, but not completely gone. A drug that produces analgesia is called an analgesic drug. Aspirin and morphine are examples. Analgesic drugs are often used in veterinary medicine to make animals with severe pain, such as postsurgical patients, more comfortable.

The Sensory System

A domestic animal's sensory system includes its skin, eyes, ears, nose, and taste buds.

All sense organs contain nerve endings that act as sensory receptors. When triggered by stimuli, sensory receptors generate nerve impulses that travel to the central nervous system, which interprets them as particular types of sensations.

An animal's sensory receptors can detect four types of stimuli:

- Mechanical (touch, hearing, balance)
- Thermal (hot and cold)
- Electromagnetic (vision)
- Chemical (taste and smell)

All of the sensations that an animal can perceive start with one or more of these four types of stimuli.

Vision

The eyes are responsible for relaying visual information from the environment to the animal. The position of the eyes varies by species, depending on whether or not they are typically predators or prey.

Figure 10.6 Prey Species

Prey species usually have their eyes positioned closer to the sides of their heads. This provides them with a wider field of vision so they can avoid predators.

Figure 10.6 Predator Species

Predators normally have their eyes positioned at the front of their heads. This helps them to accurately locate and catch prey.

The eye has three layers: an outer layer, a middle layer, and an inner layer.

Figure 10.7 Eye

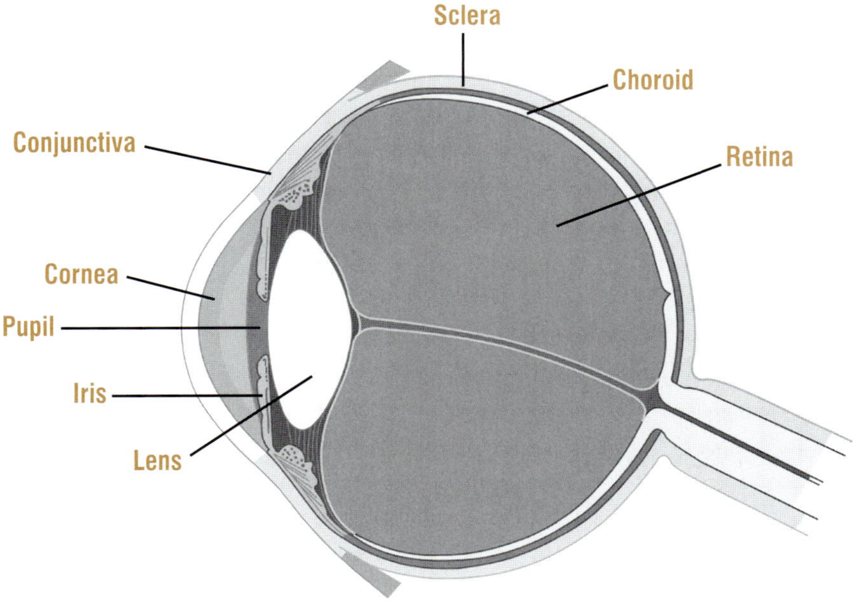

The following table summarizes the parts of the eye and their functions.

Table 10.3 Layers and Parts of the Eye

Layer	Parts	Function
Outer	Sclera, cornea, conjunctiva	Maintains the shape of the eye and provides a protective covering
Middle	Choroid, iris, pupil, lens	Provides nutrients Controls amount of light Focuses on near or far objects
Inner	Retina	Periherial vision, night vidion, color vision

Much more information about the eye can be found in *The Veterinary Assistant Career and Medical Terminology* (chapter 10, “Perception and Coordination”).

How a Visual Image Is Formed

The retina is where visual images are formed, sensed, and converted to nerve impulses that are decoded in the brain to reform the image in the conscious mind. The retina functions similarly to the film in a camera. The optic nerve is located at the back of the retina. It transmits impulses from stimulated rods and cones to the brain, allowing animals to mentally process what they are seeing.

In order for the eye to transmit a clear visual image to the brain, the image must first be formed on the retina. This is achieved by the cornea and other structures in the eye that bend or refract light rays so that they come into clear focus on the retina. The cornea does most of the work, but the lens, aqueous humor, and vitreous humor help to fine-tune the images. The image formed on the retina is actually upside down. The brain inverts the image so that the conscious mind sees everything right side up.

Hearing

For many domestic animals, hearing is a more acute sense than it is for humans. For example, dogs can detect sounds at lower and higher frequencies than people can. This is why dog whistles are effective training tools even though people cannot hear them. Dogs can also identify a sound's location faster than humans and hear sounds up to four times the distance.

The sense of hearing converts vibrations in the air into nerve impulses that are interpreted by the brain as sound. It involves the structures of the external, middle, and inner ear. The external ear funnels sound wave vibrations into the air and directs them toward the eardrum. The middle ear amplifies and transmits vibrations from the eardrum to the inner ear. The inner ear contains the sensory receptors that convert mechanical vibrations to nerve impulses.

The external ear has two parts: the pinna and the external ear canal.

Figure 10.7 Structure of the Ear

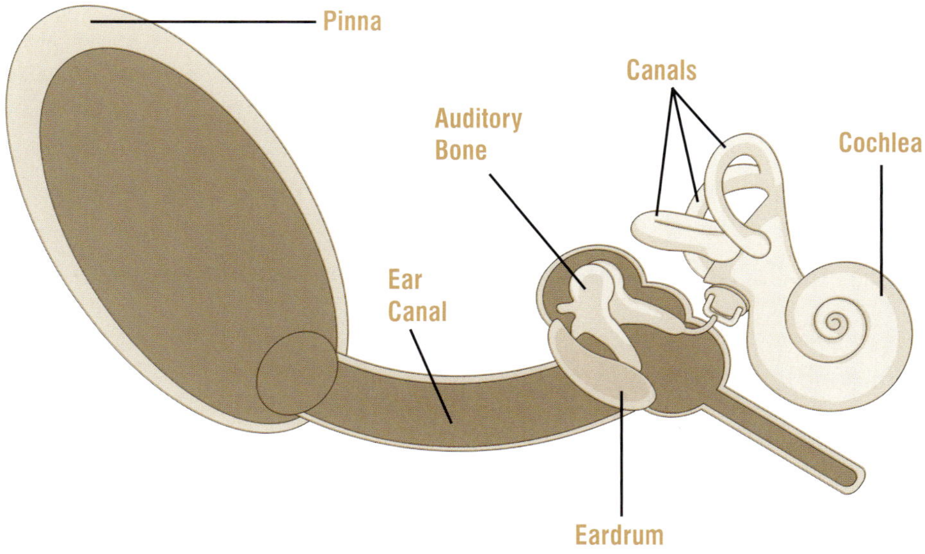

The pinna is the visible part of the ear. It is made of cartilage and covered with skin. Because domestic animals have muscles that they can use to move their pinnae, they have directional hearing. The ear canal runs from the base of the pinna to the tympanic membrane, or ear drum.

The tympanic membrane separates the external ear from the middle ear. It transmits sound waves to the middle ear by vibrating. When sound vibrations strike the tympanic membrane, it vibrates at the same frequency.

The middle ear consists of three small bones called ossicles:

- The malleus, or hammer
- The incus, or anvil
- The stapes, or stirrup

When the tympanic membrane vibrates, it sets the ossicles in motion. As they carry these vibrations across the middle ear, the amplitude of the vibrations increases. Thus, a small vibration of the tympanic membrane is all that is needed for an animal to hear a sound.

The inner ear includes three structures:

- The vestibule, which maintains balance
- The semicircular canals, which maintain balance and equilibrium
- The cochlea, the organ of hearing

The cochlea contains the organ of Corti, which converts sound waves to nerve impulses. Different sound frequencies stimulate different areas along the length of the organ. This generates nerve impulses in different parts of the organ of Corti and helps the brain to differentiate between high- and low-pitched sounds.

Taste

Domestic animals taste their food using taste buds on the tongue and palate and in the throat. Taste bud receptors respond to the chemicals in food, and then send this information to the brain along cranial nerves.

There are four main sensations of taste: sweet, bitter, salty, and sour. There is a particular area of the tongue that responds most strongly to each taste. The ability to detect many different kinds of tastes is due to combinations of the four taste sensations combined with the sense of smell.

Smell

All domestic animals have a well-developed sense of smell. Unlike people, who live in a sight-oriented world, animals often use smell to interact with their environments. For example, dogs that are out for a walk can pick up a lot of information about other dogs by sniffing the air and objects in their path.

Smell is a chemical sense that is similar to taste. Receptor cells for smell lie within the mucous membranes of the nasal cavity. Odor molecules dissolve in the mucus and come in contact with sensory receptors. These cells transmit impulses to the olfactory bulb, located under the cerebrum, which sends information related to the sense of smell from the nose to the brain. The brain then interprets an odor as a particular type of smell.

Touch

The skin contains sensory neurons that can detect chemical, mechanical, or thermal stimuli related to pressure and temperature. These receptors produce sensations of light contact, deep pressure, vibration, hair movement, heat and cold, and pain.

These nerve endings help protect animals against injury or damage by sending messages about painful sensations to the brain. When activated by a painful stimulus, the sensory neurons found in skin will cause a reflex response so that the animal will quickly remove its body part from the source of pain.

Summary

The nervous system is made up of the brain, the spinal column, and peripheral nerves. It regulates and controls all body functions.

The basic unit of the nervous system is the neuron. Neurons are specialized cells that transmit information to and from other cells in the body.

Sensory and motor information is interpreted and coordinated in the brain. The largest part of the brain is called the cerebrum. It is believed to control learning, emotions, and behavior in animals.

The peripheral nervous system is made of the cranial nerves and the spinal nerves.

It is divided into two systems:

- The automatic nervous system controls essential body functions that are not under voluntary control, such as heart rate, body temperature, respiration, and digestion.
- The somatic nervous system controls the voluntary movement of muscles.

Animals sense their environments through their eyes, ears, nose, skin, and taste buds. Information from the sensory system is transmitted to the brain, allowing the animal to respond appropriately to sensory stimuli. In general, domestic animals have well-developed senses of smell and hearing, and their vision is adapted to either the early detection of predators or the accurate location of prey.

Key Terms

Term	Definition
Automatic nervous system	Controls and regulates automatic processes related to essential body functions, such as heart rate, body temperature, respiration, and digestion. Also called the autonomic nervous system, it is subdivided into the sympathetic and parasympathetic nervous systems.
Brainstem	The part of the brain attached to the spinal cord.
Central nervous system	Comprises the brain and spinal column, which, together, control the peripheral nervous system.
Cerebellum	The part of the brain that maintains balance and posture and coordinates movement.
Cerebrum	The part of the brain that is believed to control learning, emotions, and behavior in animals. It has a right and a left hemisphere.
Cochlea	The part of the inner ear that is the organ of hearing. It converts sound waves into nerve impulses that are carried to the brain.
Cornea	The transparent part of the iris that allows light rays to enter the eye and bends them so they can be focused on the retina.
Cranial nerves	The peripheral nerves connected to the brain that transmit information between the brain and the sensory organs. Cranial nerves also control the movement of facial muscles.
Hypothalamus	Regulates body temperature, appetite, thirst, digestion, and sleeping and waking cycles.
Iris	The colored part of the eye surrounding the pupil; controls the amount of light that enters the eye by adjusting the pupil.
Lens	The part of the eye that focuses on objects.

Key Terms

Term	Definition
Nervous system	The body system comprising the brain, spinal column, and peripheral nerves, which regulates and controls all body functions.
Olfactory bulb	The organ that sends information related to the sense of smell from the nose to the brain.
Parasympathetic nervous system	The part of the automatic nervous system that brings the body back to a resting state following the fight-or-flight response to danger.
Peripheral nervous system	The network of nerves that transmit motor and sensory messages.
Pinna	The visible part of the outer ear which funnels sound waves into the ear.
Pupil	The opening at the center of the eye which determines the amount of light that enters it by changing size.
Retina	The part of the eye on which images are formed.
Somatic nervous system	The division of the peripheral nervous system that controls the movement of muscles.
Sympathetic nervous system	The part of the automatic nervous system responsible for the fight-or-flight response to perceived danger.
Tympanic membrane	The part of the ear (ear drum) that transmits sound waves to the middle ear by vibrating.
Spinal nerves	The peripheral nerves connected to the spinal cord that control the muscles and provides sensation in the neck, trunk, and limbs.
Thalamus	Receives and sends most sensory stimuli (except for smell) to the cerebral cortex, the part of the cerebrum that processes sensory information.

Answer key on page 199

What Do You Remember?

1. **The ______________ nervous system controls and regulates processes related to essential body functions.**

a. automatic
b. somatic
c. peripheral
d. central

2. **The ______________ nervous system controls the movement of skeletal muscles.**

a. automatic
b. somatic
c. peripheral
d. central

3. **_________ are the basic building blocks of the nervous system.**

a. Glial cells
b. Nerves
c. Neurons
d. Neurotransmitters

4. **The ___________ is the largest part of the brain, controlling learning, emotions, and behavior.**

a. cerebrum
b. cerebral cortex
c. cerebellum
d. brainstem

5. **The __________ is the part of the brain that maintains balance and posture and coordinates movement.**

a. cerebrum
b. cerebral cortex
c. cerebellum
d. brainstem

Answer key on page 199

What Do You Remember?

6. **The part of the eye that lets in light is the ________.**

a. pupil
b. iris
c. lens
d. retina

7. **The ________ of the eye is where visual images are formed.**

a. pupil
b. iris
c. lens
d. retina

8. **In the ear, the ________ converts sound waves into nerve impulses.**

a. cochlea
b. organ of Corti
c. vestibule
d. oval window

9. **The ________ ear amplifies and transmits vibrations from the eardrum to the ________ ear.**

a. external, middle
b. inner, middle
c. middle, inner
d. external, inner

10. **The ossicles are found in the __________.**

a. middle ear
b. inner ear
c. external ear
d. oval window

West Highland Terrier

Cat on a Fence

CHAPTER 11

The Endocrine System

Highlights of the Chapter

- Structure and function of the endocrine system
- Hormones produced by the endocrine system and their effects on the body
- Other organs that produce hormones in the body

Introduction

The endocrine system shares responsibility for coordination and control of the body with the nervous system. The two systems help maintain homeostasis in the body. As explained in chapter 1, "Introduction to Animal Anatomy and Physiology," the term *homeostasis* refers to the body's ability to regulate its inner environment to maintain normal functioning. The main difference between the nervous and endocrine systems is that, whereas the nervous system uses neurotransmitters to send instructions to muscles and glands, the endocrine system releases hormones into the bloodstream to send instructions to all body cells and tissues.

There are two types of glands in the body that secrete hormones and other products: endocrine glands and exocrine glands. Exocrine glands, such as the sweat and mammary glands, stomach, liver, and pancreas, secrete their products into ducts, and endocrine glands secrete their products directly into the bloodstream.

The endocrine system regulates metabolism, growth, development, maturation, and tissue function, and helps determine mood. It is composed of several endocrine glands, which are ductless glands

that secrete tiny amounts of hormones into the bloodstream. These hormones act like messengers, traveling to sites in the body where they find receptors to which they can attach themselves and producing effects. Each body cell has specific receptors to a variety of hormones. These receptors are like locks to which only certain keys (hormones) can fit.

Endocrine glands are found throughout the body. Table 11.1 summarizes the major endocrine glands and their hormones.

How does the endocrine system determine when to send hormones? Hormone secretion is controlled by a negative feedback system similar to how a heater is controlled by a thermostat. When room temperature falls below the temperature to which the thermostat has been set, the heater turns on and begins warming the air. When the room's temperature reaches the thermostat setting, the heater turns off.

Let's look at an example involving the thyroid gland, whose function is controlled by the anterior pituitary gland. When the thyroid hormone drops below normal levels in the body, the anterior pituitary gland releases thyroid-stimulating hormone (TSH), which stimulates the thyroid gland to produce and release more thyroid hormone. When the level of thyroid hormone in the bloodstream returns to normal, the anterior pituitary releases less TSH, causing the thyroid gland to also release less thyroid hormone.

When the endocrine system is functioning normally, there is never a shortage or oversupply of any one hormone in the body. The production and release of hormones are regulated through a negative feedback loop, which prevents over- or undersupply from occurring.

Figure 11.1 Thyroid Gland

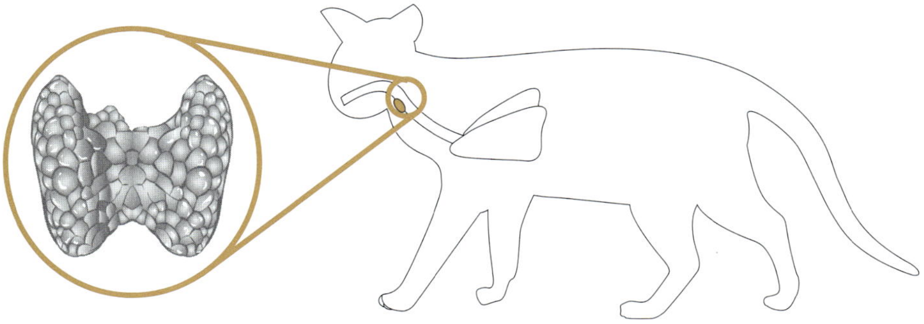

Table 11.1 Endocrine Glands and Their Functions

Gland	Hormone	Target	Action
Anterior pituitary	Growth hormone	All body cells	Growth, metabolic regulation
	Prolactin	Female mammary glands	Lactation
	Thyroid-stimulating hormone	Thyroid gland	Thyroid hormone production
	Adrenocorticotropic hormone	Adrenal cortex	Adrenocortical hormone production
	Follicle-stimulating hormone	Female ovaries	Development and maturation of ova
		Male testes	Sperm production
	Luteinizing hormone	Female ovaries	Ovulation and development of corpus luteum (structure in the ovaries that produces progestins)
	Melanocyte-stimulating hormone	Unknown	Unknown
Posterior pituitary	Antidiuretic hormone	Kidneys	Water conservation
	Oxytocin	Female uterus	Labor contractions
		Mammary glands	Milk letdown
Pineal gland	Melatonin	Brain and pituitary gland	Regulates sleep/wake cycles Causes drowsiness

Table 11.1 Endocrine Glands and Their Functions (continued)

Gland	Hormone	Target	Action
Thyroid	Thyroid hormones Calcitonin	All body cells Bones	Growth, metabolic regulation Prevents hypercalcemia (elevated blood calcium levels)
Parathyroids	Parathyroid hormone	Kidneys, intestines, bones	Prevents hypocalcemia (low blood calcium levels)
Adrenal cortex	Glucocorticoid hormones Mineralocorticoid hormones	Whole body Kidneys	Increases blood glucose Helps maintain blood pressure Retains sodium and water Eliminates potassium
Adrenal medulla	Epinephrine and norepinephrine	Whole body	Causes the fight-or-flight response
Pancreas	Insulin Glucagon	All body cells Whole body	Decreases blood glucose Increases blood glucose
Testes	Androgens (e.g., testosterone)	Whole body	Development of male secondary sex characteristics Enlargement of skeletal muscles and increased bone density
Ovaries	Estrogens Progestins (e.g., progesterone)	Whole body Uterus	Development of female secondary sex characteristics; preparation for breeding/pregnancy Preparation for/maintenance of pregnancy

The hypothalamus is a part of the lower brain that lies just above the pituitary gland. It links the conscious mind with the rest of the body by connecting higher centers in the cerebral cortex with lower brain centers and the endocrine system. This link is established through the control the hypothalamus has over the pituitary gland's activities. Blood vessels and nerves connecting the hypothalamus and pituitary gland enable the hypothalamus to control the pituitary gland's activity and, therefore, most of the rest of the body.

The hypothalamus controls the anterior and posterior parts of the pituitary gland in different ways. It controls the anterior pituitary gland by sending hormones that tell it to produce and release either more or less of a particular hormone. The hypothalamus itself produces antidiuretic hormone and oxytocin, which are transported to the posterior pituitary gland and stored. The posterior pituitary gland releases these hormones into the bloodstream when stimulated by nerve impulses from the hypothalamus.

The Pituitary Gland

The pituitary gland is often called the master endocrine gland. Many of its hormones control the activities of other endocrine glands. It does all of this despite the fact that it is the size of a small pea!

The pituitary gland is actually two separate glands with completely different functions: the anterior pituitary and the posterior pituitary. The anterior pituitary produces seven hormones when stimulated to do so by the hypothalamus. The posterior pituitary stores hormones produced by the hypothalamus and releases them when stimulated to do so.

The seven hormones produced by the anterior pituitary gland are as follows:

- Growth hormone, which stimulates body growth in young animals; also helps regulate the metabolism of nutrients in the body's cells and encourages cells to synthesize protein, providing the materials for growth and regeneration of body tissues

- Prolactin, which stimulates lactation in female animals that have given birth
- Thyroid-stimulating hormone (TSH), which stimulates the growth and development of the thyroid gland and causes it to produce its hormones
- Adrenocorticotropic hormone (ACTH), which stimulates the adrenal gland's growth and development and the release of some of its hormones
- Follicle-stimulating hormone (FSH), which causes immature ova to develop and mature in females and males to produce sperm
- Luteinizing hormone, which causes ovulation and the development of corpus luteum, a structure in the ovaries that produces the progestins required to attain and maintain pregnancy
- Melanocyte-stimulating hormone, whose function is unknown

Released by the posterior pituitary gland, antidiuretic hormone helps prevent dehydration by encouraging the body to conserve water in times of short supply. It does so by causing the kidneys to reabsorb more water back into the bloodstream instead of secreting it into urine. This makes the resulting urine more concentrated and gives it a darker yellow color and a stronger odor.

The hormone oxytocin has two targets in female animals: the uterus and the mammary glands. It causes the muscle of the uterus to contract during birthing to aid the delivery of the fetus and during breeding to help transport sperm to the ovaries. Oxytocin also causes the movement of milk down to the lower parts of the mammary gland in lactating females. This is called "milk letdown." Stimulation of the teat or nipple by nursing or milking causes oxytocin to be released into the bloodstream.

The Thyroid Gland

The thyroid gland produces both thyroid hormones (triiodothyronine and thyroxine) and calcitonin. The thyroid hormones regulate the rate at which the body's cells burn nutrients to produce energy. The production of thyroid hormone increases with exposure to cold temperatures. This increases the body's metabolic rate, which generates more heat and burns up nutrients at a faster rate. For this reason, animals housed outdoors in cold temperatures need more calories to keep warm and maintain their body weight than those kept indoors.

Calcitonin helps maintain blood calcium at normal levels. Calcium is a vital substance in the body. It is involved in many body functions, including muscle contraction, blood clotting, lactation, and the development and maintenance of bones. Calcitonin works by removing excess calcium from the blood and depositing it in bones. The bones function as the body's "calcium bank."

The Parathyroid Glands

The parathyroid glands are several small nodules located either in or near the thyroid glands. They are called "parathyroid" because of their physical relationship with the thyroid gland.

Unlike calcitonin, which prevents blood calcium levels from getting too high, parathyroid hormone prevents them from getting too low. It works by causing the kidneys to retain calcium in the blood and the intestines to absorb calcium from food. When necessary, it also withdraws calcium from bones.

Figure 11.2 Parathyroid Glands

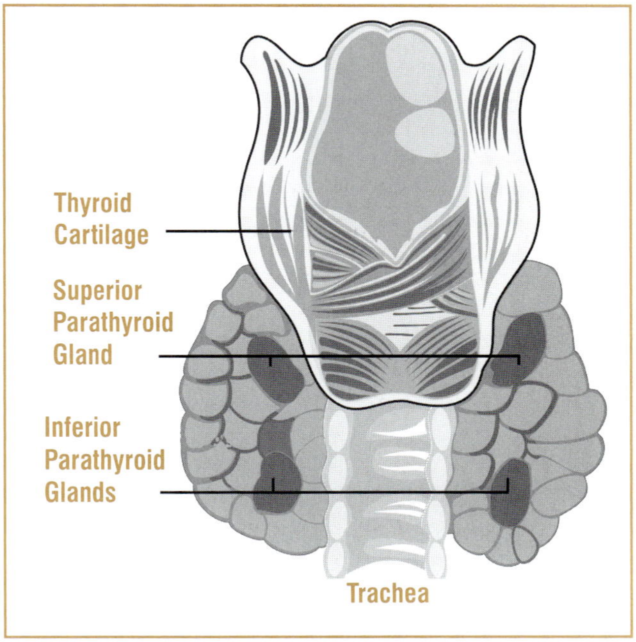

The Adrenal Glands

The two adrenal glands are named for their proximity to the kidneys (the term renal refers to the kidneys). They are located near the top of the kidneys. The two glands, which are wrapped around each other, are the outer adrenal cortex and the inner adrenal medulla. They have different functions.

When stimulated by the anterior pituitary gland, the adrenal cortex produces several different hormones, which are referred to as steroids. These include the glucocorticoid hormones, which cause blood sugar levels to rise, help to maintain blood pressure at normal levels, and help the body to withstand the effects of stress.

The mineralocorticoid hormones regulate levels of mineral salts in the body. The most important of these hormones is aldosterone, which affects the levels of sodium, potassium, and hydrogen ions. Aldosterone works on the kidneys, ensuring that sodium is reabsorbed back into the bloodstream, while potassium and hydrogen ions are excreted in urine. Although the body needs a high level of sodium to function, it needs little potassium. In fact, if too much potassium accumulates in the body, it can become toxic. Hydrogen ions affect the body's acid-base balance, so levels of this mineral must also be controlled carefully.

The adrenal medulla secretes two hormones that have similar functions: epinephrine and norepinephrine. This gland activity is controlled by the automatic nervous system, which responds to perceived threats in an animal's environment by producing the fight-or-flight response. When this response kicks in, an animal's heart rate and blood pressure increase. These effects are produced partly by the nervous system and partly by the secretion of epinephrine and norepinephrine into the bloodstream. These hormones circulate around the body to help prepare it for the intense physical activity required to deal with danger, such as predators.

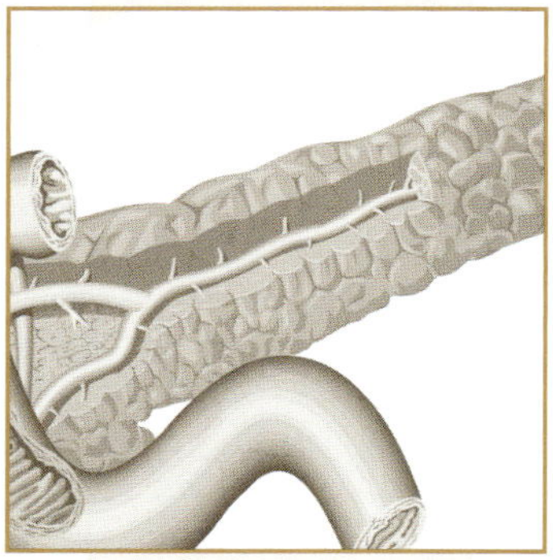

The Pancreas

The pancreas is both a digestive organ and an endocrine gland, located near the duodenum (the first part of the small intestine). Most of its mass is made up of exocrine glandular tissue dedicated to producing digestive enzymes. Tiny clumps of cells scattered throughout the pancreas, called islets of Langerhans, produce pancreatic hormones. Two of these hormones, insulin and glucagon, help control the body's use of glucose. Insulin reduces blood glucose by moving it out of the bloodstream and into cells, where it is used as fuel.

Glucagon has the opposite effect of insulin. It raises blood glucose levels by stimulating the liver to convert glycogen (a stored form of glucose) to glucose. It also stimulates the body to convert fatty and amino acids, the building blocks of fats and proteins, into glucose. Both of these actions cause blood sugar to rise. Because other hormones produced by the endocrine system also raise blood glucose levels, a deficiency of glucagon in the body is not as serious as an insulin deficiency.

The Pineal Gland

The pineal gland is a small organ in the brain, located in the deep cleft that separates the two cerebral hemispheres. The gland produces melatonin, which regulates sleep/wake cycles. The production and synthesis of melatonin is dramatically affected by light exposure to the eyes. Blood levels of melatonin are low during daylight hours and reach their peak at night, causing drowsiness. The duration of melatonin secretion each day is directly proportional to the length of the night.

Melatonin is also believed to play a role in regulating breeding cycles. The pineal gland is able to measure daylight and adjust secretion of melatonin accordingly. Melatonin affects animals' reproductive systems by inhibiting the secretion of hormones that produce sperm and ova. As days get longer in late winter, an animal's body will produce less melatonin. This helps to prepare it for the breeding season by increasing the secretion of hormones that cause sex cells to be produced.

The Testes

The two testes are housed in the scrotum. They are made up of coiled tubules where sperm are produced. They also have clumps of endocrine cells, which produce androgens, the male sex hormones, when stimulated to do so by the anterior pituitary gland. The most important androgen is testosterone, which is responsible for development of male secondary sex characteristics and sperm production. Testosterone also causes the enlargement of skeletal muscles and increased bone density in males.

Figure 11.3 Male and Female Endocrine Glands

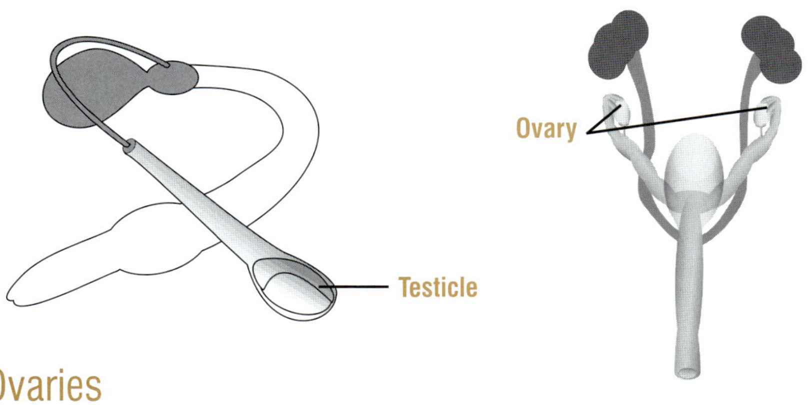

The Ovaries

The two ovaries are located in the abdomen near the kidneys. Unlike the testes, which produce sperm and hormones constantly, the ovaries produce ova and hormones in cycles. Ovarian cycles are controlled by two hormones produced by the anterior pituitary: follicle-stimulating hormone (FSH) and luteinizing hormone. The main hormones produced by the ovaries are estrogens and progestins.

Estrogens are the female sex hormones. FSH stimulates production of estrogens by causing follicles in the ovaries to develop. These follicles contain female reproductive cells that produce and release estrogens into the bloodstream. Estrogens produce the physical and behavioral changes that prepare female animals for breeding and pregnancy.

As the ovarian follicle grows, it produces more estrogen. The amount of FSH in the bloodstream decreases. The amount of luteinizing hormone, which causes ovulation, increases. Ovulation is the rupture of the follicle and the release of the ovum into the fallopian tube.

After ovulation, the high levels of luteinizing hormone in the body stimulate the cells in the empty follicle to multiply and develop into a hormone-producing structure. This is called the corpus luteum. It produces several progestins, the most important of which is progesterone. Progesterone helps prepare the uterus to receive the fertilized ovum. The hormone also maintains pregnancy once the fertilized ovum is implanted in the uterus.

If the female animal becomes pregnant, the corpus luteum is maintained in the ovary to continue producing progestins. If pregnancy does not occur, the corpus luteum shrinks and disappears and the production of progestins ceases.

Other Endocrine Organs

Hormone production is not restricted to the endocrine glands. Other organs produce hormones and work with the endocrine system to help maintain homeostasis. These include the kidneys, stomach, small intestine, thymus, and placenta.

Kidneys

In addition to filtering blood, the kidneys produce the hormone erythropoietin, which stimulates red bone marrow to increase production of red blood cells. Red blood cells carry oxygen in the blood. The kidneys produce and release erythropoietin when the oxygen content in the blood dips. They produce less of the hormone when the blood's oxygen content is high. This activity helps ensure the blood always carries enough oxygen to meet the body's need for it.

The Stomach

Cells in the stomach wall produce the hormone gastrin whenever food enters the stomach. Gastrin stimulates gastric glands in the stomach to secrete hydrochloric acid and digestive enzymes, starting chemical digestion. This hormone also causes muscles in the stomach wall to contract.

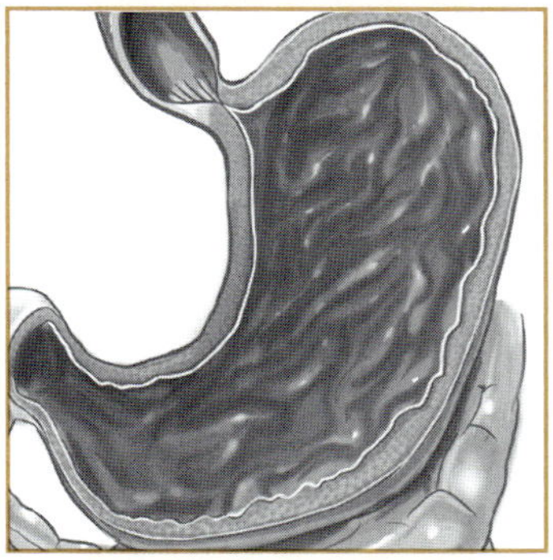

The Small Intestine

Cells in the lining of the small intestine produce two hormones when partially digested food (chyme) from the stomach enters the duodenum (the first part of the small intestine). These two hormones are secretin and cholecystokinin. Secretin stimulates the pancreas to secrete sodium bicarbonate into the duodenum to help neutralize chyme, which becomes acidic in the stomach. Cholecystokinin causes the pancreas to release digestive enzymes into the duodenum.

Both small intestine hormones act on the stomach to inhibit gastric gland secretions and stomach motility. This slows the movement of chyme into the small intestine to prevent too much food material from leaving the stomach at once. They also cause the gallbladder to contract, sending bile into the small intestine to digest fats and fat-soluble vitamins.

The Thymus

Part of the lymphatic system, the thymus is an organ that helps kick start development of a young animal's immune system. It is fairly large in young animals, but shrinks and almost disappears by the time they reach adulthood. The thymus extends along the trachea, from the level of the heart up to the larynx.

The thymus produces hormones that convert cells in the thymus and other lymph organs into the T lymphocytes or T cells discussed in chapter 5, "The Lymphatic System." T cells attack and destroy cells that have been invaded by viruses or that are cancerous.

The Placenta

The placenta is the life support system that surrounds a developing fetus during pregnancy. It connects the developing fetus to the uterine wall and supplies it with maternal nutrients. The placenta is also an endocrine organ that produces hormones that help support and maintain pregnancy. These hormones include estrogen and progesterone.

Prostaglandins

Prostaglandins are hormones that are derived from unsaturated fatty acids. They are produced in a variety of body tissues, including skin, intestines, brain, kidneys, lungs, reproductive organs, and eyes. Prostaglandins play a variety of important roles in the body. They affect blood pressure, and digestive, respiratory, kidney, and reproductive functions. Prostaglandins play a role in the contraction and relaxation of smooth muscle, the dilation and constriction of blood vessels, the control of blood pressure, initiation of inflammation in the body, and blood clotting.

Summary

The endocrine system regulates metabolism, growth, development, maturation, and tissue function, and helps determine mood. It is composed of several endocrine glands, which are ductless glands that secrete tiny amounts of hormones into the bloodstream. These hormones act like messengers, traveling to sites in the body where they find receptors to which they can attach themselves and producing effects.

The pituitary gland acts as the master endocrine gland because many of its hormones control the activities of other endocrine glands. Other endocrine glands include the thyroid gland, parathyroid glands, adrenal glands, pancreas, pineal gland, testes, and ovaries. Other organs that produce hormones and work with the endocrine system to help maintain homeostasis are the kidneys, stomach, small intestine, thymus, and placenta (in pregnant females).

Key Terms

Term	Definition
Adrenal glands	Endocrine glands that produce hormones that help maintain blood pressure and normal levels of blood glucose, water, and potassium in the body. The two adrenal glands are the outer adrenal cortex and the inner adrenal medulla.
Adrenocorticotropic hormone	Hormone released by the pituitary gland that stimulates the adrenal gland to release some of its hormones.
Aldosterone	Hormone released by the adrenal cortex to regulate mineral salts in the body.
Androgens	Male sex hormones responsible for the development of secondary sex characteristics in males and sperm production. Androgens include testosterone.
Antidiuretic hormone	Hormone released by the pituitary gland that helps prevent dehydration by causing the kidneys to reabsorb more water back into the bloodstream.
Calcitonin	Hormone released by the thyroid gland which helps maintain blood calcium at normal levels.
Endocrine glands	Ductless glands found throughout the body which produce and secrete hormones into the bloodstream.
Endocrine system	The body system of endocrine glands that regulates metabolism, growth, development, maturation, and tissue function, and helps determine mood.
Epinephrine and norepinephrine	Hormones secreted by the adrenal medulla that work with the nervous system to produce the fight-or-flight response to a perceived threat.

Key Terms

Term	Definition
Erythropoietin	Hormone produced by the kidneys which stimulates red bone marrow to increase production of red blood cells.
Estrogens	Female sex hormones that produce secondary sex characteristics in females, preparing them for breeding and pregnancy.
Exocrine glands	Glands that secrete hormones and other products through ducts. Exocrine glands include the sweat and mammary glands, stomach, liver, and pancreas.
Gastrin	Hormone produced by the stomach which stimulates gastric glands to secrete hydrochloric acid and digestive enzymes.
Glucagon	Hormone produced by the pancreas which raises blood glucose levels by stimulating the body to convert fatty and amino acids into glucose.
Growth hormone	Hormone that stimulates growth and cell reproduction.
Hormone	A chemical messenger produced by endocrine gland cells which travels through the bloodstream to other cells and tissues, where it produces its effects.
Hypothalamus	The part of the brain that controls the pituitary gland.
Insulin	Hormone produced by the pancreas that lowers blood glucose levels by moving glucose out of the bloodstream and into cells.
Melatonin	Hormone released by the pineal gland which regulates sleep/wake cycles.

Key Terms

Term	Definition
Ovaries	Female gonads that produce estrogens and progestins.
Oxytocin	Hormone released by the pituitary gland which causes the uterus to contract during birthing and milk letdown in females that are nursing young.
Pancreas	Both a digestive organ and an endocrine gland that produces insulin and glucagon.
Parathyroid glands	Endocrine glands that work with the thyroid hormone calcitonin to regulate blood calcium levels.
Pineal gland	Small endocrine gland located between the two cerebral hemispheres which produces melatonin.
Pituitary gland	The master endocrine gland, which produces many hormones that control the activities of other endocrine glands.
Progestins	Hormones produced by the ovaries after ovulation which help prepare the uterus to receive the fertilized ovum and maintain pregnancy once it occurs.
Prostaglandins	Hormones produced in a variety of body tissues that affect blood pressure and digestive, respiratory, kidney, and reproductive functions.
Testes	Male gonads that produce androgens.
Thyroid gland	Endocrine gland which produces thyroid hormones that regulate metabolism. It also produces calcitonin, which helps regulate blood calcium levels.
Thyroid-stimulating hormone	Hormone released by the pituitary gland which stimulates the growth and development of the thyroid gland and causes it to produce its hormones.

Answer key on page 199

What Do You Remember?

Match the endocrine gland with its function, listed below.

1. anterior pituitary gland
2. posterior pituitary gland
3. pineal gland
4. thyroid gland
5. parathyroid glands
6. adrenal cortex
7. adrenal medulla
8. pancreas
9. testes
10. ovaries

a. helps to regulate metabolism and lowers blood calcium

b. regulates sleep/wake cycles

c. secretes hormones that control other endocrine glands

d. raises blood calcium

e. produces fight-or-flight response

f. stimulates the kidneys to retain water in the bloodstream

g. produces female sex hormones

h. maintains blood pressure

i. regulates blood glucose

j. produces male sex hormones

Domestic Cat

Answer Key

The following are answers to the questions in the "What Do You Remember?" sections at the end of each chapter.

Chapter 1		Chapter 2	Chapter 3			Chapter 4	Chapter 5
1–1	1–2		3–1	3–2	3–3		
1. a	1. c	1. d	1. a	1. b	1. b	1. a	1. d
2. c	2. h	2. a	2. b	2. e	2. g	2. d	2. a
3. a	3. d	3. c	3. d	3. a	3. i	3. c	3. b
4. a	4. a	4. d	4. c	4. c	4. j	4. c	4. d
5. b	5. k	5. d	5. d	5. d	5. h	5. b	5. d
6. d	6. b	6. c	6. a		6. c	6. d	6. a
	7. g	7. d	7. b		7. d	7. b	7. d
	8. f	8. a			8. e	8. d	
	9. j				9. a		
	10. c				10. f		
	11. i						

Chapter 6	Chapter 7	Chapter 8	Chapter 9	Chapter 10	Chapter 11
	7–1				
1. c	1. a	1. f	1. b	1. a	1. c
2. a	2. c	2. g	2. d	2. b	2. f
3. d	3. d	3. a	3. a	3. c	3. b
4. c	4. a	4. h	4. d	4. a	4. a
5. d	5. c	5. e	5. b	5. c	5. d
6. b	6. c	6. i	6. a	6. a	6. h
7. c	7. d	7. d	7. c	7. d	7. i
8. b	8. a	8. b	8. d	8. b	8. j
				9. c	9. j
				10. a	10. g

7–2

Simple Carbohydrate	Complex Carbohydrate	Complex Carbohydrate and Protein	Only Fat	Both Fat and Protein
apples	potatoes	soybeans	peanut oil	beef
sugar	wheat	peas	corn oil	eggs
honey	rice			cheese
				chicken
				milk

Friesian Stallion